ADULT AUTISM ESSENTIALS:

A STEP-BY-STEP APPROACH TO NAVIGATING RELATIONSHIPS, PROFESSIONAL LIFE AND FINDING RESOURCES WHILE CELEBRATING OUR STRENGTHS

JASON JONES

TABLE OF CONTENTS

INTRODUCTION

It is estimated that over 5 million adults in the U.S. live with autism. Despite this significant number, the unique challenges and strengths of adult autism remain primarily overshadowed by the focus on childhood diagnoses. This book is born out of the urgent need to shift the spotlight, emphasizing the rich, often untapped potential of adults like us.

At the heart of this book is a commitment to empower you. Whether you're navigating the nuances of an autism diagnosis yourself or you're a family member, friend, or professional seeking to provide support, this guide is not just a general resource but a tailored tool designed to illuminate the path ahead. It's centered on understanding, leveraging resources, and fostering positive narratives about adult autism, specifically for you.

This book is comprised of clear, focused chapters. Each section builds on the last, starting with a foundational understanding of autism in adulthood, moving through practical coping strategies, and culminating in how to access and optimize support systems.

The approach is practical and positive, designed to recognize and amplify your inherent strengths.

Inclusivity and diversity are the cornerstones of the discussion here. Autism manifests uniquely across different individuals, and this book respects that spectrum, aiming to address a broad array of experiences, needs, and aspirations. By integrating the latest research and evidence-based practices, the guidance you'll find is relevant and actionable. Real-life examples and expert opinions enrich the narrative, ensuring the insights are relatable and scientifically sound.

This is not just a book about the challenges of living with autism; it's a celebration of potential. It's about understanding that with the right tools and mindset, every adult with autism can lead a fulfilling life.

I invite you to engage with this material openly, apply what you learn, and expand the conversation about adult autism. Let this book be a stepping stone beyond coping into thriving.

As we turn this page together, let me share a message of hope and encouragement: every day, strides are made in understanding and supporting adults with autism. With this book, you're not just staying informed but moving forward. Here's to discovering the incredible journey that awaits you.

UNDERSTANDING ADULT AUTISM

D id you ever stop to think that maybe your quirky Uncle Joe, who's obsessed with train schedules, or your friend Lisa, who can't stand loud noises, might be navigating life on the autism spectrum? It's easy to miss because when we talk about autism, it's usually all about the kids. But hey, kids grow up, right? And adults with autism continue to live, grow, and face challenges that the world often overlooks. This chapter is like that first sip of coffee in the morning—eye-opening, slightly bitter, but ultimately invigorating—as we explore what it means to be an adult navigating the world with autism.

DEFINING AUTISM IN ADULTS: BEYOND CHILD-CENTRIC VIEWS

Clarifying Misconceptions

It's a familiar scene: discussions about autism are bustling with talks of early intervention, school support, and helping children thrive. But what happens when these children grow up? Often, the support fades away, the resources become scarce, and the conversation stops. Adults with autism haven't outgrown their diagnosis; they've grown into adults with autism. It's crucial to understand that the signs and challenges of autism evolve rather than disappear with age. For instance, while a child might have frequent meltdowns due to sensory overload, an adult might experience intense anxiety in similar situations, affecting everything from social interactions to employment.

Adult-Specific Challenges

Now, let's talk about the elephant in the room: societal expectations. As an adult, you're expected to get a job, socialize like a pro, and manage many different adult responsibilities. For someone with autism, these tasks are challenging rather than routine challenges. Navigating social norms at work, managing sensory overload during a crowded networking event, or simply keeping up with the relentless pace of daily adult life can be daunting. These are not just quirks but significant hurdles that can impact one's quality of life and mental health.

The Lifelong Nature of Autism

The truth is that autism doesn't come with an expiration date. It's not a subscription service you can cancel once you reach adulthood. Acknowledging that autism is a lifelong condition is pivotal. This recognition is not just about individual support but the urgent need for societal integration and respect for neurodiversity across all ages. It's about shifting the narrative from merely coping to thriving, from surviving to living fully, and it's a call to action for all of us.

Case Study: Meet James

Let's talk about James. Diagnosed with autism at 30, James spent years baffled by his difficulties in social settings and his intense focus on subjects like meteorology. Before his diagnosis, he often felt like a square peg being forced into round holes. Post-diagnosis, armed with understanding and adjustments in his approach to work and relationships, he's not just functioning—he's flourishing. James's story is a testament to why recognizing adult autism is crucial; it's not just about slapping on a label. It's about transforming lives through understanding and tailored support.

Interactive Element for Reflection

Jot down the environments you find most challenging. Next to each, write what could make it more manageable. This simple exercise can help you start thinking about practical changes that can significantly impact daily functioning and quality of life.

As we peel back the layers of what it means to be an adult with autism, it becomes clear that this isn't just a topic for textbooks and doctors' offices. It's about real people living real lives with unique challenges that deserve our recognition, understanding, and action. It's about fostering an inclusive and supportive society where everyone can thrive.

THE SPECTRUM EXPLAINED: UNDERSTANDING VARIABILITY IN AUTISM

Imagine walking into an ice cream shop thinking you're just going to find the usual suspects—vanilla, chocolate, and strawberry—but instead, you discover an entire range from mango jalapeño to lavender honey. That's a bit like diving into the understanding of the autism spectrum. It's not just a few flavors—a whole spectrum with a rich variety that can profoundly affect perception, experience, and interaction with the world.

No two people on the autism spectrum are alike, and each has a unique pattern of behavior and level of ability. For instance, some might excel in visual and music arts but find social interactions and verbal communication challenging. Others, like a human calculator, might be great with numbers and patterns but may need help with physical coordination. This variability means that each individual needs a tailored approach to learning, working, and socializing that plays to their strengths and supports their challenges.

Let's break down a couple of real-life scenarios to illustrate this variability. Consider Missie, a brilliant pharmacy technician known for her attention to detail but finds office banter and loud environments overwhelming. Then there's Mark, who has a phenomenal memory for facts and dates, which makes him a star in his history class; however, he struggles with anxiety in social situations and prefers scripted conversations to spontaneous ones. These examples highlight that being on the spectrum can encompass many skills and challenges, not just deficits.

Common stereotypes often paint all individuals with autism with the same brush, suggesting they all have savant skills or cannot form emotional connections, which is far from the truth. The reality is very different and more enjoyable. We can better appreciate each person's individuality by challenging these stereotypes and understanding the spectrum. Recognizing this variability helps provide appropriate support and enriches our perspective, allowing us to enjoy each person's unique contributions.

So, the next time you hear someone mention the autism spectrum, remember the vast range of abilities and challenges it encompasses. Please think of the unique individuals behind the label, each with their strengths, preferences, and needs, navigating the world uniquely.

LATE DIAGNOSIS: CHALLENGES AND RELIEF IN DISCOVERY

Imagine you've spent your life feeling like you're constantly missing a memo that everyone else got. You've always felt offbeat in a world that plays a rhythm you can't quite catch. Then, one day, you stumble upon a piece of the puzzle that makes everything click—a late diagnosis of autism. It's like finding out there's a reason why the music never made sense. The following emotional rollercoaster can swing from relief and validation to confusion and frustration. Getting diagnosed with autism in adulthood isn't just a medical event; it's a redefining moment that reshapes understanding of oneself and recalibrates every past interaction and experience.

For many, this discovery comes with a massive sigh of relief. It's common to hear, "Now I understand why I've always felt differently." This revelation often clarifies a lifetime of misunderstood behaviors and emotional responses. Suddenly, the challenges with social cues, hypersensitivity to sensory inputs, or deep dives into interests make sense. However, the journey toward this clarity isn't devoid of hurdles. The path to a late diagnosis is often littered with misdiagnoses, from anxiety to personality disorders, leading to years of ineffective treatments and therapies. The lack of early support means that many have had to navigate life's challenges without the right tools, often developing complex coping mechanisms that may not be entirely effective or healthy. That was certainly the case for me as a younger adult. It wasn't until I had my child with autism that I realized I was probably on the spectrum.

Moreover, the entrenched habits and coping strategies developed over the years can be hard to adjust. These routines and behaviors, once essential for managing undiagnosed autism, may no longer serve their purpose and can be difficult to unlearn. The shift from self-perceived "oddness" to a recognized medical diagnosis can also stir a range of emotions, from relief to resentment for the years spent in the dark.

Yet, amidst these swirling emotions and challenges, a late diagnosis opens a new realm of possibilities. For the first time, tailored support becomes accessible, from therapies that address specific aspects of autism to communities that resonate with shared experiences. This support not only fosters self-understanding but also enhances the quality of life. Knowing the "why" behind differences allows for more effective strategies in work, relationships, and social interactions. It paves the way to finding one's tribe—the community with similar struggles and triumphs. Engaging with this community can be profoundly affirming, providing a sense of belonging many have missed.

If you're contemplating seeking a diagnosis or have recently discovered you're on the spectrum, the importance of professional guidance cannot be overstated. Navigating the complex terrain of adult autism requires a nuanced understanding that qualified professionals can provide. They can offer clarity in the sea of confusion that often accompanies the process, helping to differentiate between autism and other conditions that might mimic its symptoms. They also play a crucial role in pointing you toward the right resources and support systems, ensuring that the path ahead is aligned with needs that are now understood better.

Engaging with professionals doesn't just end with obtaining a diagnosis; it extends to learning how to adapt to and integrate this new understanding into your life. Whether it's exploring therapies to refine social skills, pursuing strategies to manage sensory overload, or simply finding ways to embrace and celebrate your unique perspective, the guidance you seek now can redefine your future. It's about building a life that acknowledges and accommodates your autism, not one that forces you to mask or hide it. This newfound knowledge is a powerful tool—it's up to you to wield it wisely and carve out a more comfortable space for yourself in a world that now makes a little more sense.

NEURODIVERSITY: EMBRACING DIFFERENT COGNITIVE ABILITIES

Imagine entering a garden where every flower, bush, and tree is identical. It's a world devoid of color, shape, and scent. Now, envision a garden teeming with a kaleidoscope of colors, various shapes, and a symphony of scents. That's the beauty of diversity— it's vibrant, fascinating, and makes life much richer. This concept isn't just about flora; it applies to human brains, too. That's where neurodiversity comes into play. Neurodiversity is the idea that neurological differences among people are just differences. These are not defects to fix but variations that should be acknowledged, respected, and celebrated, much like natural diversity.

Now, let's talk about how this relates to autism. Autism is one of many neurological conditions, including ADHD, dyslexia, and others, that manifest uniquely across different individuals. Embracing neurodiversity means recognizing that people with autism experience and interact with the world in ways that are not wrong or less valid, just different. It's about moving away from the idea of "curing" autism and, instead, promoting acceptance and support, creating a society that appreciates and utilizes the strengths of all brains, not just the typical ones.

The impact of embracing neurodiversity on society is profound, especially when considering areas like education, employment, and social interactions. In educational settings, recognizing neurodiversity leads to more inclusive practices. It can mean the difference between a child supported in their learning journey versus one continually marginalized. In the workplace, embracing neurodiversity can lead to a more productive and satisfied workforce. Neurodiverse-friendly practices can include everything from flexible work environments to tailored communication strategies, allowing individuals to perform at their best. Socially, understanding neurodiversity can foster more empathetic and accommodating interactions between all people, reducing misunderstandings and conflicts caused by neurological differences.

But don't take my word for it. Consider the words of Michael, a software developer with autism, who shared, "In my team, they value my detail-oriented nature and my unique approach to problem-solving. They see these as strengths, not hindrances. It's empowering." And there's Lisa, a graphic designer, who said,

"Knowing that my workplace supports my need for a quiet space and structured tasks makes a huge difference. It means I'm not just surviving—I'm thriving."

These voices from the community highlight the tangible benefits of accepting and supporting neurodiversity. They underscore the potential for individuals to excel when their neurological differences are acknowledged and embraced. This approach doesn't just change lives for those on the spectrum; it enriches the social fabric of our communities, enhancing creativity, innovation, and empathy. It shifts the narrative from one of seeking conformity to celebrating the unique contributions each person can make.

Embracing neurodiversity is about more than being nice. It's about recognizing the true spectrum of human capability and designing our social structures to accommodate and nurture this diversity. It's a movement toward a more inclusive, innovative, and compassionate society. So the next time you think about diversity, remember it's not just what's on the outside that counts. The diversity of the mind is a hidden gem that, once recognized, can be the source of incredible enrichment and progress.

SENSORY PROCESSING IN ADULTS: MANAGING OVERLOAD

Imagine you're at a bustling city market. There's a symphony of sounds: vendors shouting, music playing, kids crying. Now multiply the volume by ten. Throw in lights that flicker so intensely; it feels like a strobe light at a rave, and the scents are so strong you can taste them. Welcome to a day in the life of someone with sensory processing issues. For adults with autism, the world can often feel overwhelming, like living in a perpetual state of sensory assault that others might only experience in extreme situations. Sensory processing issues mean that the brain has a unique way of responding to everyday sensory information. This can include being hypersensitive to textures, sounds, and lights or not being sensitive enough, like not noticing changes in temperature or bodily sensations.

Managing these sensory overloads isn't just about comfort—it's about being able to function. Take, for example, the simple act of going to work. For someone hypersensitive to sounds, the clatter of a busy office can be paralyzing. For this, noise-canceling headphones can be a game-changer. They muffle the overwhelming background noise, allowing focus and productivity to take the front seat. On the flip side, for those who need more sensory input, something as simple as a textured fidget toy can provide enough stimulation to maintain concentration. These tools are necessities that can significantly alter an adult's ability to navigate daily life successfully.

But it's not just about tools; it's also about strategies. One practical approach is creating a "sensory diet"—a personalized plan incorporating activities and accommodations tailored to manage an individual's sensory needs throughout the day. This could mean scheduling quiet breaks between meetings, using desk lamps with softer light, or accessing a private space when the sensory input becomes too much. It might require creating an environment where sensory inputs can be controlled and adjusted to meet personal comfort levels, thus reducing the likelihood of sensory overload.

Now, let's talk impact. Sensory issues can turn a typical day at work or a simple social gathering into a minefield. Social interactions often involve unpredictable sensory variables, whether the restaurant noise or a crowded street's chaotic visuals. For someone with sensory processing issues, these environments can trigger feelings of anxiety and discomfort, making social engagements something to endure rather than enjoy. It affects not just social life but mental health, contributing to increased stress and anxiety and, in some cases, can lead to social withdrawal.

Advocating for accommodations is crucial, whether in the workplace or social settings. It starts with open conversations about sensory needs and educating those around you about what adjustments can make a significant difference. It's about shifting the narrative from demanding special treatment to facilitating inclusive environments where everyone can perform at their best. Whether requesting a quiet workspace away from the noisy open office layout or asking friends to hang out in a more peaceful, less sensory-intense environment, these adjustments help manage sensory overload effectively.

In every scenario, the goal is to reduce the sensory load to a manageable level so that adults with autism can engage with the world in a way that minimizes stress and maximizes their potential. It's about understanding that sensory processing issues are as much a part of the neurological landscape as the need for glasses might be in the visual realm. Just as you wouldn't expect someone with poor vision to navigate a visually cluttered environment without corrective lenses, we shouldn't expect those with sensory sensitivities to cope without appropriate accommodations. Equipping individuals with what they need to succeed turns overwhelming worlds into manageable environments where they can be successful.

EXECUTIVE FUNCTIONING: STRATEGIES FOR DAILY MANAGEMENT

So, let's talk about executive functioning. Imagine you're the conductor of an orchestra, but instead of musicians, you're trying to manage what feels like an impossible amount of daily tasks that can't seem to play in tune. That's a bit like dealing with executive functioning challenges as an adult with autism. Executive functioning is our mental control room—it's where we plan, prioritize, multitask, and manage time. For many adults on the spectrum, this control room can feel a bit like it's been hit by a whirlwind, especially when faced with the demands of everyday adult life.

Now, you're not alone if you find yourself frequently overwhelmed by tasks, struggling to keep up with schedules, or perpetually feeling like you're playing catch-up. These challenges are common, but they are manageable. One effective strategy is harnessing technology to keep things in check. For instance, smartphone apps that manage reminders and to-do lists can be lifesavers. They take the guesswork out of what needs to be done and when. It's like having a personal assistant in your pocket, nudging you gently about that meeting tomorrow, or reminding you to pick up milk on the way home.

Another game changer is breaking tasks into smaller, more manageable steps. Consider the daunting task of organizing a big event or even just cleaning out your garage. Instead of looking at it as one gigantic mountain to climb, break it down into foothills. Today, list what needs to be done for the event or sort through one box in the garage. Tomorrow, pick the following small task. This approach can transform an overwhelming chore into small, achievable victories.

Creating structured environments is also crucial. Structure doesn't mean rigidity; it's about creating a predictable framework that helps guide your day-to-day activities. This could mean establishing set times for meals, work, exercise, and leisure or organizing your living space in a way that makes sense to you and reduces chaos. Think about it like setting up a series of signposts and guardrails on your daily road trip, making the journey smoother and less stressful. For me, it's trying to stick to a rigid schedule during the week and using reminder notes to keep track of my daily tasks.

Let's draw inspiration from people who've turned these strategies into triumphs. Take Emily, a graphic designer who found her niche in creating visually stunning work but struggled with meeting client deadlines. By using a digital planner that mapped out each step of her projects, she not only improved her time management but also reduced her work-related anxiety. Her clients noticed the difference, too, leading to more projects and boosting her professional confidence.

Then there's Alex, who always felt overwhelmed by the prospect of social gatherings. By breaking down each event into planned stages—preparing conversation topics ahead of time, setting time limits for how long he'd stay, and arranging a quiet space to retreat if needed—socializing became less daunting. This structured approach allowed him to enjoy gatherings more and gradually improve his social interactions.

With the right strategies, managing executive functions is possible. Whether leveraging technology, breaking tasks down, or creating structured environments, the key is finding what works best for you.

The goal isn't to strive for perfection but to make everyday tasks and responsibilities more manageable, reducing as much stress as possible while enhancing your ability to navigate the complexities of adult life. While the control room might get messy sometimes, you have the tools and strategies to get things back on track, one small step at a time.

PRACTICAL COPING STRATEGIES

Navigating the adult world with autism every day can feel like you're trying to solve a Rubik's Cube that someone keeps painting over. It's complex, colorful, and constantly changing. However, you've got some excellent skills, and with the right strategies, you can manage this. This chapter includes a collection of practical, real-world strategies designed to help you navigate sensory challenges, enhance your social interactions, and create a life that's not just functional but fantastic. Ready to dive in? Let's start with something essential: crafting your sensory diet.

CREATING A PERSONALIZED SENSORY DIET

What's on Your Sensory Menu?

Think of a sensory diet as your playlist of activities that help you manage how you experience the world around you. It's not about food but rather about feeding your senses with the right stimuli that keep you feeling balanced and alert. Just like you might crave a hearty bowl of spaghetti after a long day or a crisp apple to wake you up, your nervous system craves specific sensory experiences to function at its best.

Tuning into Your Sensory Needs

First, let's figure out what your senses are yearning for. This isn't about passing a test or meeting someone else's standards. It requires getting accurate with how different environments and activities make you feel. Start by keeping a simple journal. Note times when you feel unusually agitated, anxious, or can't seem to focus. What was happening around you? Loud noises? Bright lights? Conversely, write down when you feel calm and collected. Was it during a hot shower or perhaps wrapped in a cozy blanket? This is critical data collection on what works for YOUR sensory system.

Crafting Your Sensory Diet

Now, with your trusty journal insights, outline your daily sensory diet. This includes deliberately planning soothing and stimulating activities throughout your day to keep your sensory balance in check. Do you love the calming effect of heavy blankets? Consider starting your day with a few minutes under a weighted blanket to ease into the morning. Are you overwhelmed by the bustle of your commute? Consider including noise-canceling headphones paired with your favorite tunes or a fascinating podcast to control the sensory overload.

The Art of Adjustment

Even with the best-made plans, life likes to throw curveballs. What works today might not work tomorrow, and that's okay. Your sensory diet isn't set in stone. Regularly revisiting and tweaking your sensory diet is vital. Maybe you've started a new job, and the office has different lighting affecting you, or you've discovered a new hobby that calms you more than you expected. Adjustments are part of the process. It's like being a DJ for your own life, constantly mixing the tracks to keep the mood just right.

Visualizing Your Day: A Sensory Map

Let's create a sensory map of your day to give you a clearer picture. Visualize your typical day from morning to night, and plot out when and where you might encounter sensory challenges. Next to each challenge, note a strategy from your sensory diet that might mitigate these. This map prepares you for potential sensory pitfalls and empowers you to take control of your environment in a way that supports your well-being. It's about making your day work for you, not the other way around.

By tuning into your sensory needs, crafting a personalized sensory diet, and becoming adept at making adjustments, you're setting yourself up to succeed. Remember, this is about understanding and working with your unique sensory blueprint, not fitting into a mold. So, go ahead, experiment, adjust, and enjoy the process of discovering what makes your sensory world tick.

TECHNIQUES FOR ENHANCING SOCIAL INTERACTION SKILLS

Imagine that you are at a social event, and everyone seems to be effortlessly mingling while standing there, wondering if there's a manual for starting a conversation without sounding like you're reciting a weather report. Sound familiar? Well, you're not alone. Navigating social interactions might not come as naturally to you as to others, but guess what? It's a skill; like any skill, it can be honed with practice and a few tricks up your sleeve.

Let's start with the basics: reading social cues, turn-taking in conversations, and understanding body language. Think of social interactions as a dance. They know when to step forward, when to spin, and when to let their partner lead, which can make the difference between stepping on toes and gliding smoothly across the dance floor. Start by observing. Pay attention to how people react when you speak. Do they lean in, smile, or nod? Great! These are green lights. Keep doing what you're doing. If they're glancing away, checking their phones, or looking over your shoulder, take it as a cue to adjust the topic, ask them a question, or give them space to chime in.

Role-playing can be a game-changer here. It might feel awkward initially, but practicing conversations with a trusted friend or in front of a mirror can boost your confidence. Try different scenarios—ordering food at a restaurant, asking for directions, or making small talk at a party. Focus on your tone, your facial expressions, and your body language. This kind of practice can desensitize you to the anxiety of real-world interactions and make them feel more manageable.

Now, let's talk tech. In this digital age, apps and online platforms are designed to help you practice social interactions. These can range from virtual reality environments to chat apps that connect you with others looking to improve their social skills. These platforms provide a safe space to experiment with different ways of communicating, allowing you to mess up in a space with a reset button—a luxury not often available in real life.

Building confidence in social settings isn't just about practicing skills; it's also about changing the way you talk to yourself. The chatter in your head can be your best ally or worst critic. Engage in positive self-talk. Remind yourself of your strengths, your past successes, and your potential. Before stepping into a social scenario, give yourself a mental pep talk and boost your confidence like you're the main character in your movie. And when you're out there, remember that everyone has insecurities. Most people are too caught up in their social anxieties to focus on yours.

Gradual exposure is also crucial. Start small. Strike up a conversation with a barista, a coworker, or a neighbor. Build up from there. Each positive interaction, no matter how small, is a building block toward greater confidence. Over time, these interactions will feel less daunting and more like another part of your day.

Enhancing your social skills is like a journey. Each step poses new challenges but also brings new skills and more confidence. Keep going, keep learning, and remember that you've got this. After all, the social world is just another arena, and you're getting better equipped every day.

NAVIGATING WORKPLACE DYNAMICS WITH AUTISM

Sometimes, it can feel like the workplace is like a jungle gym for adults—full of twists, turns, and sometimes a few too many monkey bars. When you're navigating this playground with autism, things can get even trickier. You have unique strengths, but sensory issues, time management struggles, and social etiquette demands can make the 9-to-5 grind feel more like a 9-to-9 marathon. What is the best way to maneuver through this mess? Let's break it down, starting with your legal rights because, believe it or not, the law is on your side!

Understanding Your Legal Rights

First, knowing your workplace rights is essential and is your responsibility. Laws such as the Americans with Disabilities Act (ADA) ensure that individuals with disabilities, including those with autism, can request reasonable accommodations at work. These aren't just niceties; they're your rights. Accommodations might include a quieter workspace, flexible scheduling, or the right to wear headphones to minimize sensory overload. The key here is the word "reasonable"— making adjustments that help you perform your job without causing undue hardship to the employer. It's about optimizing everything possible to ensure you can give it your best shot.

Communicating Your Needs

How do you bring up these accommodations without setting alarm bells or sharing your medical history? By being transparent and professional. Start by deciding what accommodations you need to enhance your productivity. Then, have a chat with your HR department or supervisor. You don't need to disclose your diagnosis if you're not comfortable. Instead, focus on how the adjustments can boost your performance. For instance, instead of saying, "I need a quiet space because I get overwhelmed by noise due to my autism," you might say, "I've found that I perform best in a quieter environment. Could we explore possible solutions to help me maintain my productivity?" It's like negotiating a better seat at a concert—not because you want special treatment, but because you know where you'll enjoy the show best.

Strategies for Common Workplace Challenges

Handling the day-to-day challenges in the workplace is next. Say the break room feels like a Vegas casino, or meetings are more draining than a marathon. Here's where your personalized strategies come into play. For noisy environments, noise-canceling headphones can be a lifesaver. When managing your time, tools like visual timers or apps that break your work into focused intervals can help keep you on track without feeling overwhelmed. And for those dreaded social functions? Have a game plan. Decide how long you'll stay, prepare some conversation starters, and permit yourself to take a break when needed. You don't have to avoid challenges but can manage them on your terms.

Real-Life Success Stories

Need a little inspiration? Let's talk about Sam, who works in graphic design. Sam found the open-office plan at his job overwhelming. After a chat with his manager, he moved to a quieter corner and got permission to wear noise-canceling headphones. His productivity soared. Then there's Priya, an IT specialist, who struggled with shifting priorities and last-minute changes at her job. She worked with her team to develop a more transparent communication system, allowing her to prepare for changes and manage her tasks more effectively. Sam and Priya used their understanding of their needs and rights to create a work environment where they could excel and maximize their strengths.

Navigating workplace dynamics with autism doesn't have to feel like a solo expedition in the wilderness. With the proper knowledge of your rights, clear communication, tailored strategies, and inspiration from those who've walked this path, you can turn your work experience into an adventure. Remember, you can create a space where you shine, using your unique abilities to their fullest. Clear a path to a workplace where you feel valued, understood, and capable.

STRATEGIES FOR REDUCING ANXIETY IN PUBLIC SPACES

Ever felt like you're about to give a speech in front of thousands, but all you're doing is stepping out to grab coffee? For those of us with autism, public spaces can sometimes feel overwhelming. There are several strategies to reduce anxiety in these public arenas. Let's unpack them one by one.

First up, let's talk preparation. It's your secret weapon. Before stepping out, spend a few moments planning your trip. This doesn't mean you need a detailed blueprint, but knowing where you're going, the route you'll take, and what you might encounter can ease anxiety. Use apps to check the busiest times for public places and plan your visit accordingly. Maybe the local café is less crowded in the late morning than at lunchtime. Knowing this can help you choose the best time to go. Also, pinpoint potential sensory triggers. If you're sensitive to noise, you might want to avoid times when places are busiest. Have an exit strategy, too—know where the quiet spots are, or plan something comforting post-visit, like a walk in a peaceful park, to decompress.

Now, let's discuss coping mechanisms for when the anxiety creeps in despite the best-laid plans. Focused breathing is a classic: breathe slowly through your nose, hold for a few seconds, then release through your mouth. Repeat until you feel calmer. There are also sensory tools like fidget spinners or stress balls. Keep one handy. They're not just toys but items that help redirect your nervous energy.

Tolerance to crowded or noisy environments is like building muscle—it takes time and practice. Start small. Maybe today you spend five minutes in a moderately busy place, and tomorrow you spend ten minutes. Pair these outings with something positive. Maybe post-visit, you treat yourself to your favorite snack or an episode of your favorite show. This positive reinforcement makes the experience less about the stress and more about the reward. Gradually, these places might still be challenging but won't feel as daunting.

Lastly, having a support system can be immensely reassuring. If going alone feels too much, have a friend or family member join you. Choose someone who understands your challenges and can offer a calming presence. Consider carrying an alert card—a simple card explaining your autism and that you might need assistance or patience. It's a discreet way to seek help without explaining your situation verbally in a moment of stress.

By preparing adequately, having your coping mechanisms ready, gradually increasing your tolerance, and ensuring support, navigating public spaces can become a more manageable and enjoyable part of life. Remember, the goal here isn't to eliminate anxiety; it's to manage it so you can enjoy more of the world around you. With these strategies in your back pocket, every outing can become a step toward reclaiming your comfort in public spaces. So, next time you step out, remember that you're not just going out—you're gearing up for a smoother, more enjoyable experience.

TOOLS FOR EFFECTIVE COMMUNICATION IN RELATIONSHIPS

How can we communicate in relationships when the world speaks a different language? For those on the autism spectrum, a conversation's usual ebb and flow can sometimes feel like trying to read a book with half the pages missing. It's not just about what is said but how it's said. Understanding that the communication styles between individuals with autism and neurotypical folks can be as different as sushi and hamburgers is crucial. One is not better than the other; they're just different flavors of interaction.

People with autism often lean toward direct and literal communication. For us, the beauty of a clear, straightforward statement is like a breath of fresh air in a smoggy city. We thrive on clarity. However, neurotypicals often prefer a more subtle or nuanced approach, with a layer of social coding that can seem cryptic. Imagine you're decoding a secret message where "That's an interesting idea" might mean, "I don't agree, but I don't want to be rude." It's like being in a play where everyone else has the script, and you're performing improv. Recognizing these differences is the first step in bridging the communication gap. Understand that when misunderstandings arise, it's not because anyone is doing it wrong; it's just a matter of translation.

Conflict in relationships is like garlic in cooking; a little bit can bring out the flavors, but too much can be overwhelming. For many of us, conflicts can feel like personal attacks, but they don't have to. This is where the magic of "I" statements comes in.

Instead of saying, "You never listen to me," try, "I feel upset when I think I'm not being heard." This slight tweak in phrasing can change defensive standoffs into opportunities for understanding. It's like switching from throwing rocks to offering a hand. Pair this with active listening—where you focus on hearing not just the words but the emotions behind them—and you will be able to turn conflicts into conversations.

Expressing needs and setting boundaries is an important topic to discuss. It's about being clear about your emotional property lines and inviting others to respect them. Let's say you need some time alone after work to decompress, not to push people away but to pull your peace close. Here's a simple template you can use: "I feel [emotion] when [situation]. I need [action or change]." For example, "I feel overwhelmed when there's a lot of noise after I get home. I need some quiet time to settle in." It's straightforward, respectful, and transparent. Setting boundaries isn't building walls; it's laying down guidelines that help everyone coexist more comfortably.

Enhancing empathy in relationships often involves stepping into someone else's shoes, even if they don't quite fit. For those on the spectrum, understanding others' emotional worlds can sometimes feel like trying to read a book in a language we don't fully understand. But, just like learning any language, it gets easier with practice. A great exercise is what I call "Emotion Charades." With a partner, take turns acting out emotions without words and try to guess each other's feelings. This adds a bit of fun and sharpens your ability to read emotional cues. Another helpful technique is sharing stories of times you both felt similar emotions like excitement, sadness, or frustration. This helps understand the emotion and see how your partner experiences and expresses it. It's like comparing notes in class; you can see what you missed and share what you picked up.

By mastering these steps—clarifying communication styles, navigating conflicts with grace, articulating needs clearly, and fostering empathy—you equip yourself to have healthier relationships. It's about turning misunderstandings into opportunities for growth, conflicts into deeper connections, and conversations into shared journeys of understanding. So, let's keep the dialogue going, the boundaries respected, and the empathy flowing. After all, relationships are not just about finding the right person but also about being the right person, and with these tools, you're well on your way to building meaningful, fulfilling connections.

BUILDING AND MAINTAINING ROUTINES FOR STABILITY

Imagine life as a series of dominoes lined up perfectly. With one slight nudge, everything flows smoothly from start to finish, with predictability and order. That's the beauty of a well-oiled routine, especially for someone with autism. Routines are like mental maps, helping you navigate the day without the stress of the unknown. They provide a structure that can reduce anxiety by making the world more predictable and less chaotic.

Think about how comforting it feels knowing what's coming next in your day. No surprises, no sudden changes that send your stress levels through the roof—just a clear path laid out in front of you. This predictability is particularly calming for adults with autism. You're in control, and that control can make all the difference in how you experience your day. It's not just about sticking to a schedule; it's about crafting a day that aligns with your needs, allowing you to function at your best.

Now, let's get into creating effective routines. Start by mapping out your typical day: what tasks need to be done, what activities you enjoy, and what responsibilities you have. Then, weave these into a daily and weekly plan that balances work, personal time, social activities, and rest. It might look like setting specific meal times, work tasks, exercise, and downtime. Maybe mornings are for creativity, afternoons are for social interactions, and evenings are for unwinding. The key is consistency. Like a favorite TV show, having a predictable lineup can give you something to look forward to and prepare for.

However, life isn't a sitcom, and unexpected plot twists are part of the game. This is where flexibility comes into play. While the idea of a routine might seem rigid, building in buffers for unexpected changes can keep you from feeling thrown off when things don't go as planned. Maybe it's as simple as having free time blocks that can be adjusted as needed or setting up "if-then" scenarios in your plan. For example, "If my afternoon meeting gets canceled, I'll use that time for a walk or to catch up on reading." This kind of planning doesn't just prepare you for changes; it empowers you to handle them easily, reducing potential stress.

Let's discuss some tools to help keep your routines on track. Digital planners and apps are fantastic for this. They can send you reminders, help you track your tasks, and adjust your schedule. Look for apps that allow you to visualize your day with color-coded blocks of time, making it easy to see what's on your agenda at a glance. Some apps also offer flexibility in scheduling, which is perfect for incorporating those necessary buffers. These digital tools are like having a personal assistant in your pocket, always ready to help you manage your day.

By understanding the benefits of routines, creating a balanced and flexible schedule, and utilizing tools to maintain it, you're setting yourself up for success. Routines can transform overwhelming chaos into manageable order, making each day more straightforward. Remember, the goal is to make life smoother, not confine you to a rigid framework. So, tailor your routines to fit your life, not vice versa.

As we wrap up this chapter on practical coping strategies, from crafting a sensory diet to managing workplace dynamics and navigating social interactions, remember that each plan offers a stepping stone toward more significant autonomy and fulfillment. They're about making your world bigger, brighter, and more manageable. Keep these strategies in hand as we progress and continue adapting them to fit your evolving needs and experiences. Next, we'll dive deeper into emotional well-being and mental health, exploring how to maintain balance and peace in a world spinning too fast.

EMOTIONAL WELL-BEING AND MENTAL HEALTH

Have you ever felt like your brain is a browser with about a hundred tabs open? Some are blaring music, others are quietly loading, and there's always that one that's frozen. That's a little of what navigating life with autism can feel like, especially when it comes to managing anxiety. But here's the good news: just like you can manage those browser tabs, you can also manage anxiety. You'll come to know which tabs to close, which to mute, and which to expand into full-screen mode.

IDENTIFYING AND MANAGING AUTISM-RELATED ANXIETY

Recognizing the Triggers

First off, let's play detective and spot what triggers anxiety. For many adults with autism, familiar villains include sensory overloads—like that overly bright room or the constant hum of city traffic—and daunting social situations that feel like you are doing stand-up comedy on a bad day. It's understanding what flips your anxiety switch. Start by keeping a simple anxiety journal. Write down when you felt anxious and note what was happening around you. Was it noisy? Were there too many people? Did plans change at the last minute? This isn't just busy work; it's crucial intel. Knowing your triggers is half the battle, as it allows you to prepare, avoid, or adjust your strategies to keep anxiety at bay.

Techniques for Managing Anxiety

Now, it is time to equip you with an arsenal of techniques for anxiety. Deep breathing exercises are like hitting the reset button for your nervous system. It's surprisingly effective at calming those jitters. Cognitive-behavioral techniques are also gold. They help you challenge and change thoughts of "This is going to be a disaster" to something more balanced, like "I'm prepared, and I can handle this." Then there's structured problem-solving, which involves breaking down a worry into manageable chunks and tackling it step by step rather than letting it grow into a monster under your bed.

Personalized Anxiety Management Plans

Not all strategies work for everyone, so you need your personalized anxiety management plan. This plan is your playbook for tricky days. It includes known triggers, techniques that have worked for you, and a list of activities that boost your mood (like listening to your favorite album or a walk in the park). Incorporate regular check-ins with yourself to update the plan as you discover more about what works and what doesn't. Think of it as constantly updating your favorite playlist; the more you fine-tune it, the better it gets.

Professional Support Options

Sometimes, though, you need to bring in the big guns, and that's where professional help comes in. Therapists, especially those experienced in working with adults on the autism spectrum, can be invaluable. They're like having a guide in a foreign city—they can help you navigate confusing areas and introduce you to new strategies, like mindfulness or therapy using art or music, which you might not have considered. If you're thinking about treatment, look for professionals who specialize in treating patients on the autism spectrum. They get the nuances and can often offer the most tailored strategies. Remember, seeking help is not a sign of defeat; it's a sign of being smart about your mental health.

Interactive Element: Anxiety Journal Template

To get you started on identifying your triggers and managing your anxiety, here's a simple template for your anxiety journal.

1. Date/Time:
2. Where I was/What I was doing:

3. Sensory environment (noisy, bright, etc.):
4. Social setting (alone, with friends, in a crowd):
5. What I felt (describe your anxiety symptoms):
6. Possible triggers:
7. Coping strategies I tried:
8. What helped? What didn't?

This journal isn't just a place to vent; it's a tool for transformation. Use it to become more attuned to your needs and more adept at handling the challenges that come your way. Each entry is a step toward understanding and mastering your anxiety, not just for today but for all the tomorrows to come. It's a journey of self-discovery and growth. Each entry brings you one step closer to a more peaceful and fulfilling life.

DEPRESSION: RECOGNIZING SIGNS AND SEEKING HELP

Depression is the ultimate party crasher. It sneaks in uninvited and can flip your world upside down. Now, for those of us on the autism spectrum, depression can wear some pretty convincing disguises—like suddenly finding your usual routines exhausting or feeling less chatty than a mime at a library. It's tricky because sometimes these changes are subtle; they creep in like shadows at dusk, making them hard to spot. But recognizing these signs is crucial because depression in adults with autism doesn't always wave the classic red flags that we see in neurotypical folks.

For starters, emotional expression might not be your go-to communication style. Maybe you've mastered keeping a poker face while feeling like a storm is raging inside. This masking can make it challenging for those around you to notice something's off. Changes in routine are also significant clues. If you're suddenly skipping meals, avoiding your favorite weekly comic book meetup, or if the systems and schedules that are your bread and butter start feeling like chains, these could be distress signals from your brain.

Depression can be a voracious beast, gnawing away at your mental and physical health. It's like walking around with a backpack full of rocks; it weighs you down, making everything from getting out of bed to socializing impossible. This hefty load can strain your social ties, transform your living space into a fortress of solitude, and turn daily responsibilities into overwhelming obstacles. The ripple effect can touch every corner of your life, often amplifying the sensory and social challenges that come with being on the autism spectrum.

Alright, so how do you arm yourself against this invisible adversary? With knowledge and therapy. Navigating the healthcare labyrinth to find the proper support can be daunting, but it's a quest worth embarking on. Start with your primary care provider—they can guide you toward specialists who get the whole picture, not just a slice. When it comes to therapy, think of it as finding a new ally. Therapists specializing in autism can offer tailored strategies that mesh with how you see the world. They're like custom-tailored suits; they fit you perfectly and comfortably and make you feel invincible.

You mustn't just settle for the first therapist you meet. It's okay to shop around. Think of it as test-driving cars. You wouldn't buy the first one you see, right? You want the one that feels right, where you can sit back, open up, and not feel judged. And sometimes, alongside therapy, you might explore the option of medication. This isn't for everyone, and it's not a magic pill, but for some, it's crucial for their mental health. It's like having that extra boost when the hills get steep. And just like any tool, it works best when it's the right fit, carefully monitored by medical professionals who are in tune with your needs.

Remember, reaching out for help isn't a sign of weakness; it's a strategy for strength. It's about assembling your team and setting out on the path to reclaim your life from the clutches of depression. So, take that first step. Pick up the phone, make that appointment, and start the conversation. Your mental health is worth fighting for, and believe me, you're not alone in this battle.

THE IMPACT OF EMOTIONAL REGULATION ON RELATIONSHIPS

Imagine you're at a bustling party, and suddenly, someone bumps into you, spilling your drink. Your initial impulse might be to snap or storm off, but then, you take a deep breath, count to ten, and laugh it off instead. That is emotional regulation in action— managing difficult human emotions, especially within the intricate dance of relationships.

Emotional regulation is about understanding and managing your emotions so they don't manage you. Think of it as the thermostat of your emotional world, helping you adjust the temperature to keep your environment comfortable and your interactions smooth. For adults on the spectrum, mastering this can be particularly challenging due to emotional and sensory input's intense and often overwhelming nature. However, the payoff in personal and professional relationships is worth the effort.

Emotional triggers in relationships can range from a misunderstood comment to feeling overwhelmed by social expectations. Recognizing these is your first step. Pay attention to the moments when your stress levels spike or your mood plummets. What's happening around you? Who's involved?

Tracking these will help you predict and prepare for them in the future, reducing the chances of emotional surprises.

Relaxation techniques such as guided imagery can be lifesavers during high-tension moments. Picture this: before responding to a heated conversation, you visualize a serene beach or slowly tense and relax your muscles from head to toe. These techniques can help shift your brain from a fight-or-flight response to a more composed state, allowing you to approach the situation with a cooler head.

Structured problem-solving is another invaluable practice. When faced with an emotional problem, break it down into manageable parts. Identify the problem, brainstorm possible solutions, weigh their pros and cons, and decide on an action. This systematic approach can help demystify overwhelming emotions.

Let's sprinkle in some real-life magic with a couple of case studies. Consider Jenna, a software developer who often felt misunderstood by her colleagues, leading to frequent frustration and anger. By recognizing her triggers—usually moments when her ideas were dismissed without discussion—Jenna implemented a "pause and plan" approach. She would take a brief walk, use deep breathing techniques, and then return to the conversation with clear, calm feedback on her ideas. This improved her relationships at work and reduced her overall stress levels, making her daily interactions more pleasant and productive.

Then there's Mark, who found social gatherings overwhelming, often leading to abrupt exits that confused his friends. By understanding his need for regular breaks from sensory and social stimulation, Mark began to schedule "time-outs" during gatherings to regroup emotionally. This simple strategy allowed him to enjoy socializing more. He explained his needs to his friends, deepening their understanding and support.

The role of a solid support system in managing emotional regulation cannot be overstressed. Friends, family, and therapists can provide a sounding board for your feelings, offer reassurance, or give constructive feedback when your emotional responses might not match the situation. Just knowing there's someone who understands and supports your efforts at emotional regulation can make a world of difference. It's like having a team of cheerleaders who celebrate your successes and help you regroup when things don't go as planned.

Incorporating these strategies into your daily life improves your ability to handle emotions effectively. It enriches your relationships, creating a more understanding, supportive, and connected network of people around you. As you continue to practice and refine these techniques, your emotional regulation becomes more instinctive. This makes life easier and more fulfilling, one emotion at a time.

SELF-CARE PRACTICES FOR STRESS REDUCTION

What exactly is self-care? We're not just discussing bubble baths and scented candles (I can't lie-I LOVE scented candles!). Self-care is your maintenance checklist that keeps the machine—aka you— running smoothly. For adults with autism, proper self-care practices are crucial not only for managing stress but also for enhancing overall mental health.

Self-care can look different for everyone, especially in the autism community, where sensory sensitivities can make the typical advice a bit tricky. It requires finding activities that fit like a glove, tailored to your needs and preferences. Engaging in special interests can be a fantastic way to reduce stress. Whether collecting stamps, sketching quietly, or unraveling the mysteries of the universe through books, these activities aren't just hobbies—

they're your escape from the world's chaos. They allow you to dive deep into what you love, providing a sense of accomplishment and joy that can be a balm for everyday stresses.

Structured relaxation techniques also play a pivotal role. This might include guided meditations that don't just help you relax but are also tailored to sidestep sensory pitfalls like overwhelming narrations or background music. Progressive muscle relaxation can be another great tool, where you systematically tense and relax different muscle groups. This technique helps reduce physical tension and brings a heightened awareness of bodily sensations, which can be particularly beneficial if sensory processing is challenging.

Physical activities are equally important; we're not necessarily talking about marathons. You can incorporate gentle, sensory-friendly exercises into your routine. Maybe it's yoga focusing on deep, calming breaths or a solitary evening walk in a quiet, familiar park. These activities support both physical health and mental well-being. They act as a natural stress reliever. Plus, they can be adjusted to whatever level feels good for you—no need to push beyond what makes you comfortable.

Creating a Self-Care Routine

Establishing a self-care routine that you can stick to is like setting the rhythm for a dance that makes you feel alive, not tires you out. It should blend seamlessly into your daily life, ensuring it's sustainable and doesn't feel like just another chore. Start by identifying times in your day when self-care can be naturally integrated. Are you a morning person? Maybe that's the perfect time for some light stretching or a few pages of your book. Do you find your routine lagging after lunch? That could be your cue for a brief walk or tea in a calm corner.

The key here is consistency mixed with flexibility. A routine helps automate these practices, making them part of your day without needing constant decisions or willpower. However, life is unpredictable, and flexibility is your friend. Sometimes, you might need to swap out one activity for another or adjust the timing. The goal is to maintain a flow that feels refreshing rather than rigid.

Monitoring and Adjusting Self-Care

Keeping a pulse on how effective your self-care routine is and making adjustments is essential. Regular check-ins with yourself are crucial. How are you feeling emotionally and physically? Are there activities that once soothed you but now feel like they're missing the mark? You may need to recalibrate and evolve your strategies to match your current needs.

Sometimes, a minor tweak can make a huge difference. Maybe it's changing the time of day you engage in a particular activity or introducing something new that aligns better with your current situation. The adjustment process is ongoing, a perpetual fine-tuning of mechanisms that support your well-being.

Embracing self-care is about building a relationship with yourself in which you regularly check in, assess your needs, and adjust as necessary. It's not selfish; it's essential, a core component of your mental health that keeps you feeling balanced, energized, and ready to face whatever comes your way. So take that time, dive into your interests, stretch your muscles, and clear your mind. You're not just doing it to feel good now—investing in your future self, ensuring you're as strong, centered, and ready as possible for the adventures ahead.

USING MINDFULNESS TO ENHANCE EMOTIONAL CLARITY

Mindfulness. What a buzzword it has become, right? But strip away the trendiness, and you're left with a genuinely transformative practice, incredibly potent for individuals navigating the sensory and social intricacies of autism. Think of mindfulness as the art of being present, fully engaged with the here and now, not lost in regrets of the past or worries about the future. It's about experiencing life momentarily with a gentle, open, and accepting attitude. This can be a game-changer for those on the spectrum, offering a way to dial down the sensory static and tune into what matters in the present.

So, how does mindfulness work its magic? It starts with the breath. Mindful breathing is your anchor in the often-stormy seas of sensory and social overload. Try this: sit quietly, close your eyes, and take a slow, deep breath through your nose, feeling your chest expand and your belly rise. Hold it for a moment. Now, exhale slowly through your mouth, imagining tension melting away with the breath. This simple practice can help center your thoughts and calm your body, making it an excellent tool when the world feels too loud, bright, or fast.

But mindfulness isn't just about breathing. It extends to mindful observation and listening, which can transform everyday experiences. Break it down: mindful observation involves noticing the details around you without judgment. The next time you take a walk, try to see the colors of the leaves, the patterns of the clouds, the dance of light and shadows. It's not just a walk anymore; it's an exploration, a moment-to-moment encounter with the world in vivid detail. Then there's mindful listening, which means listening to understand, not to respond. In conversations, this can help you tune into the nuances of tone, emotion, and meaning, making interactions less about stress and more about connection.

Integrating mindfulness into daily life doesn't require you to meditate for hours or sit silently on a mountaintop. It's about weaving mindfulness into the fabric of your day. Start with routine activities—like brushing your teeth or washing dishes—and approach them with full attention. Notice the sensations, the movements, the sounds. Turn the mundane into moments of mindfulness, transforming routine into something richer and more profound.

Now, if you're thinking, "Sounds great, but how do I dive deeper?" there are plenty of available resources. Books like *The Miracle of Mindfulness* by Thich Nhat Hanh offer a gentle introduction to the practice. At the same time, apps like Headspace and Calm provide guided meditations tailored to various needs, including stress reduction and focus improvement. For those who prefer a structured learning environment, mindfulness courses, often available through community centers or online platforms, can offer detailed guidance and support.

Embracing mindfulness is like learning a new language—the language of your sensory and emotional landscape. It doesn't just help manage the challenges of autism; it enhances the quality of every moment, making life more vibrant, colorful, and enjoyable. Whether you're trying to navigate a crowded store, engage in conversation, or give yourself peace on a hectic day, mindfulness offers a way to reset, refocus, and recharge. It's a pathway to a more present, peaceful, and pleasant life. So, why not give it a try? The present moment is a pretty incredible place to be.

THERAPY OPTIONS: WHAT WORKS FOR AUTISM?

Navigating therapy options can sometimes feel like ordering coffee at one of those fancy cafés where the menu looks more like a science equation. Let's simplify the menu today and explore the array of therapeutic modalities that can cater to the nuanced needs of autistic adults. Each therapy type is like a different coffee blend; you might have to taste a few before you find the one that hits the spot.

Cognitive Behavioral Therapy (CBT) is popular, starting with the classics. It's like the espresso of therapies—solid and effective, particularly good at helping manage anxiety and depression by challenging and changing unhelpful cognitive distortions and behaviors. Then there's Behavioral Therapy, which focuses more on modifying harmful behaviors and reinforcing desirable ones. Think of it as your straightforward, no-frills Americano; it gets the job done without too much complexity.

However, the world of therapy has been brewing some intriguing blends. For instance, therapies like Social Skills Therapy are specifically designed to enhance social understanding and interaction. This therapy type works through role-playing and direct instruction to build up those skills, making social interactions less of a chore and more of a choice.

Therapies like neurofeedback are popular these days. This technique is fascinating; it involves training your brain by showing real-time displays of brain activity, kind of like having a Fitbit for your brain. It helps understand and regulate your brain's activity, potentially reducing anxiety symptoms and improving concentration. Another innovative therapy is Integrated Play Therapy, which uses the universal language of play to help express feelings, modify behavior, develop problem-solving skills, and relate to others. It's particularly significant if traditional talk therapy feels too stiff.

Choosing the right therapy and therapist is crucial—it's like finding your favorite café where the barista knows your order by heart. It's essential to consider your specific needs, symptoms, and personality. For instance, a therapist who offers a sensory-friendly environment would be a better match if you're highly sensitive to sensory input. Don't hesitate to ask potential therapists about their experience with autism and their approach. Therapy is a personal experience, and the right fit can make all the difference.

Self-advocacy in therapy is your right. It involves speaking up about your needs, asking questions, and actively participating in your therapeutic journey. Remember, you are the expert on your own life. If a particular approach isn't working, it's okay to voice that and explore alternatives. A good therapist will respect and encourage this dialogue.

When exploring therapy options, remember that the goal is to enhance your quality of life. It's about making the daily grind more manageable and helping you connect with your strengths. Therapy can be a powerful ally in navigating the challenges of autism. It can significantly improve how you feel and interact with the world.

As we wrap up this chapter on emotional well-being and mental health, remember that managing mental health is not about eliminating challenges but equipping yourself to handle them more effectively. From understanding anxiety and depression to mastering self-care and mindfulness and finding the proper therapeutic support, each step you take is a move toward a more balanced and fulfilling life. As we continue, be ready to adapt and apply them as you grow and change. The mental health journey is ongoing, and with each step, you become better equipped to handle what life throws your way.

NAVIGATING RELATIONSHIPS

Welcome to the wild world of relationships, where navigating through family dinners, roommate drama, and the occasional "Who left the milk out?" can feel like a full-season reality TV show. Now, throw autism into the mix, and the plot thickens! Relationships, with all their nuances and subtleties, can be tricky for anyone. Still, when you're wired to interpret the world differently, those everyday interactions can turn into a series of "did they mean this or that" moments. This chapter is about turning those confusing daily interactions into a straightforward, readable guide—tailored just for you.

AUTISM IN THE FAMILY: DYNAMICS AND UNDERSTANDING

Examining Family Roles

Everyone plays a part in the grand theater of family life: the protector, the nurturer, the jester, and sometimes, the mystic who seems to operate on a different wavelength—that might be you, and that's perfectly fine. Autism can shuffle these roles in ways that are both challenging and enriching. It might mean you need more alone time, which can be puzzling to the family protector who wants to engage more. Or perhaps your attention to detail and memory of facts can turn you into the family historian, a role that brings its expectations. Families, like all dynamic systems, need to adapt and adjust. It's about finding a balance where everyone's needs are acknowledged. This might mean setting new traditions that consider sensory sensitivities or redefining success in ways that aren't solely based on social milestones but on personal growth and happiness.

Communication Strategies

Communication is the art of turning thoughts into words that others can understand. This can get mighty tangled in families! Clear and effective communication within the family can often bridge many misunderstandings. Here's a strategy: plain speaking. This means saying what you mean and meaning what you say without the fluff or ambiguity that can lead to misunderstandings. Encourage your family to adopt this clear communication style, explaining that this helps you interact more effectively. Visual aids can be a game-changer, too. Think about using charts or apps to organize family chores or schedules. These can help clarify expectations and reduce the stress of miscommunication, making family life more like a well-oiled machine rather than a game of charades where everyone's guessing the rules.

Support from Family Members

Support is a two-way street that requires giving and taking in equal measure. Educating your family about how autism affects you can open doors to support that's both meaningful and specific. It's essential to help them understand why you might need to skip that noisy family gathering or why you follow certain religious routines. At the same time, they need to know how to offer support without crowding you. Establishing boundaries is critical. Maybe it's having a sign on your room door when you don't want to be disturbed or setting designated times to discuss household matters. Remember, it's okay to say no or need space, and it's equally OK to ask for help when overwhelmed. It's about building a support system that respects autonomy while ensuring everyone pulls together.

Navigating Changes

Life is about change—new jobs, moving houses, relationships beginning or ending—and these transitions can be difficult, especially when routines are your anchor. These events can feel daunting, whether moving out for the first time, considering marriage, or embarking on a new career path. Family can be your grounding force during these times. Discuss your concerns and the support you'll need to navigate these changes. Planning is your ally. Create transition plans considering your sensory and communication needs and involving your family. Whether visiting a new home several times before moving in or discussing potential changes in family dynamics due to marriage, these strategies can help demystify the unknown and smooth transitions.

In navigating the complex web of family relationships, remember that every family is a unique blend of personalities, challenges, and strengths. Your autism adds another layer to this blend, bringing challenges and incredible insights. By fostering clear communication, understanding roles, supporting each other appropriately, and managing transitions with care, you can cultivate a family life that's not only manageable but profoundly enriching. Now, let's continue exploring the other facets of relationships, each with its challenges and triumphs.

DATING AND AUTISM: FINDING COMPATIBILITY

The dating scene can sometimes feel like you're trying to solve a 1,000-piece puzzle blindfolded. And when you're on the autism spectrum, it might seem like the puzzle keeps adding more pieces. But here's the good news: the dating world has evolved, and there are now more pathways than ever to help you find someone who gets you and cherishes your unique way of experiencing the world. So, let's unwrap some strategies that can make navigating the dating scene less complicated and much more fun.

First, let's talk about where to meet potential partners. Traditional settings like loud bars or bustling parties can often be "Sensory Overload Central." Instead, consider platforms and places that align more closely with your comfort zone. Online dating can be a great starter. Sites like Hiki, a dating and friendship app specifically for the autistic community, or even more mainstream platforms like OkCupid, which allows for detailed profiles and pre-meeting chats, can help ease the pressure. These platforms enable you to express yourself in writing, which can be less daunting than an immediate face-to-face conversation. Plus, they allow you to get to know someone before diving into real-time interactions, helping you gauge compatibility.

Communication, as always, is critical, especially when expressing your needs and expectations. Being upfront about autism in your dating profile or early conversations can be empowering when you're on the spectrum. It sets the stage for transparency and filters out individuals who might not understand your unique way of interacting with the world. Share what environments are comfortable for you, your preferred communication style, and what a good relationship looks like. Think of it as setting the rules for the game early on so everyone is on the same page.

Now, recognizing compatibility and spotting red flags can be daunting. It's important to know what works for you in a relationship. Maybe you need someone patient who gives you time to process your thoughts and feelings, or perhaps someone who shares similar sensory sensitivities or interests. Pay attention to how potential partners react when you discuss autism. Do they seem curious, open, and supportive? Great signs! Are they dismissive, overly critical, or uncomfortable? Big red flags. Remember, compatibility isn't so much finding an exact match; it is discovering someone who appreciates your unique traits and whose company feels comfortable, not challenging.

Lastly, let's talk about self-confidence. In the dating world, being yourself is your greatest strength. Trying to "fit in" or mask certain traits might be tempting, but authenticity is vital to finding meaningful connections. Embrace your quirks—they make you, you. Plus, confidence is attractive. Accepting and loving yourself shows and sets the foundation for someone else to appreciate and love you for who you are. Whether it's your deep knowledge of

18th-century literature, your unmatched Tetris skills, or how you can recall every detail of your favorite movie series, these are not just fun facts but the threads of your unique tapestry. Flaunt them.

Navigating the dating world with autism doesn't have to be a solitary quest. With the right platforms, clear communication, an eye for compatibility, and a solid dose of self-love, you can turn dating into an exciting journey to find someone who understands your world and wants to be part of it. Let your authentic self shine.

EFFECTIVE COMMUNICATION WITH NON-AUTISTIC PARTNERS

So, you've found someone special who makes your heart sing a bit louder, and they're neurotypical. That's fantastic! However, navigating a relationship where you and your partner process the world differently can sometimes feel like dancing to different tunes. One of the best ways to fix this is by mastering the art of communication. It's not just about talking more; it's about talking smart.

Bridging communication styles between partners with and without autism starts with understanding that you both might interpret and express thoughts and feelings in distinct ways. You might appreciate blunt, direct communication, while your partner might rely more on emotional cues or implied meanings, which can be as clear as mud to you. Here's a tip: develop a "communication codebook." This could be a literal document or just a mental note of phrases and their meanings and cues that each of you might commonly use. For instance, if your partner says, "Do you want to leave the party?" they might ask, "Can we leave now? I'm noticing you're feeling overwhelmed." Over time, this codebook can help clarify your dialogues, turning misunderstandings into understanding.

Negotiating sensory needs is another tune to harmonize. Maybe crowded places or loud environments that barely register for your partner hit you like a ton of bricks. It's crucial to communicate these sensory preferences and needs openly. Start by explaining your sensory thresholds—what's okay, what's challenging, and what's a definite no-go. Then, work together to find compromises that respect these needs without confining your partner's social life. Maybe agree on a signal for when you feel overwhelmed in public or plan outings during quieter times. Remember, it's about finding a balance where you feel comfortable and respected.

Setting boundaries goes hand-in-hand with good communication. It's like drawing a map that shows where the treasure is buried but also marks out the danger zones. Communicate your needs for personal space, routine, or specific interactions. Perhaps you need a heads-up before being brought into large gatherings, or maybe unplanned changes throw you off. Express these needs calmly and clearly, and discuss how your partner can help respect these boundaries. In turn, inquire about their boundaries, too. This mutual understanding fosters respect and minimizes friction, making your relationship's ground firmer.

Now, on to regular check-ins. These are not just "How was your day?" conversations but structured times to discuss deeper needs, challenges, and progress in your relationship. Think of it as a relationship tune-up. During these check-ins, ask each other open-ended questions like, "How have you felt about our communication this past month?" or, "Is there something I can do better to support you?" These discussions can help prevent minor misunderstandings from becoming more significant and ensure both partners feel heard and valued. It helps maintain the health of your relationship proactively, providing both of you are pulling in the same direction.

Navigating a relationship where different neurotypes meet can be like blending various musical genres. It might take some tuning, a bit of give and take, and a lot of listening, but the result can be a beautiful harmony that plays a tune unique to the two of you. So, keep those lines of communication open, respect each other's needs and boundaries, and keep checking in.

BUILDING FRIENDSHIPS ON SHARED INTERESTS

Let's discuss friendships. Finding and maintaining friendships is difficult enough, especially when you throw autism into the mix. But here's a little secret: your special interests, which you're incredibly passionate about, can be the golden keys to unlocking meaningful friendships. Whether it's your unmatched knowledge of vintage comic books, your knack for coding, or your love for gardening, these passions are not just hobbies; they're potential connectors to like-minded souls.

Leveraging Special Interests

Imagine your interest as a beacon, sending signals to potential friends who share your enthusiasm. The first step is putting yourself in physical and digital places where these interests are shared. Local clubs, workshops, and conventions can be great starting points. Online forums and social media groups centered around your interests abound. The beauty of connecting over shared interests is that it gives you an instant common ground, a foundation to build a conversation. It lessens the pressure to navigate the small talk that sometimes feels like wading through a swamp. Engaging in activities related to your interest also provides a natural structure to interactions, which can be a comfort if spontaneous socializing feels overwhelming.

Social Skills for Friendship

Social skills like reciprocity and active listening are the glue that holds friendships together. Reciprocity means giving back as much as you take in a relationship. It's like a game of catch—you've got to throw the ball back for the game to continue. In friendship terms, it means showing interest in your friends' lives, not just sharing your experiences. Listening skills are equally crucial. Active listening involves hearing what the other person is saying and showing that you value their words. It's not just about waiting for your turn to speak; it's about truly engaging with their stories, asking follow-up questions, and expressing empathy. And remember, friendships are not just about deep, meaningful conversations; they're also about sharing fun and laughter, so feel free to let your guard down and enjoy simple, light-hearted activities together.

Online Communities

In today's digital age, the world is literally at our fingertips, including access to vibrant communities where you can make connections that transcend geographical boundaries. Online communities can be particularly appealing if face-to-face interactions are overwhelming or your interests are niche. Platforms like Wrong Planet and various Facebook groups provide safe spaces where you can interact with others who understand the nuances of autism. These platforms often have threads dedicated to specific interests, from technology and science to art and literature, making it easier to find and connect with individuals who share your passions. Participating in these communities can also boost your confidence, helping you hone your social skills in a relatively low-pressure environment.

Maintaining Friendships

Friendships, like plants, need care to grow. Over time, managing expectations and maintaining communication can determine whether a friendship thrives or withers. Be clear about what you can offer in a friendship and what you hope to receive. This might mean discussing how often you're comfortable meeting up or what activities you prefer. Regular check-ins can help keep misunderstandings minimal and ensure both parties feel valued. Conflict is a natural part of any relationship, but handling it honestly and respectfully strengthens bonds rather than breaks them. If disagreements arise, approach them with a problem-solving mindset. Express your feelings clearly without placing blame, and be open to hearing the other person's perspective. This approach not only resolves conflicts but also deepens mutual understanding and respect.

Building and maintaining friendships as an adult with autism might require some extra tools and strategies, but the rewards— genuine connections and shared joy—are universally understood. Whether you're bonding over a mutual love for medieval poetry, collaborating on a coding project, or supporting each other through life's ups and downs, these friendships can enrich your life in countless ways, adding colors to your spectrum that you might not have realized were missing. So, take the leap, reach out, engage, and let your shared interests pave the way to friendships that reflect who you are.

HANDLING CONFLICTS: PRACTICAL TIPS FOR ADULTS WITH AUTISM

Conflict is as inevitable as taxes and just about as enjoyable. When you toss autism into the mix, navigating the choppy waters of disagreement can feel more like steering a canoe in a storm. Understanding the dynamics and learning to manage conflicts can turn these dreaded encounters into opportunities for growth and understanding, both for you and the people you interact with.

Let's break down the typical conflict dynamics, especially when one or more individuals involved have autism. We experience the world uniquely, including how we process communication and emotions. Misunderstandings can arise when these unique perspectives clash with more typical ways of expressing or interpreting information. For instance, you might prefer straightforward communication and find indirect hints or sarcasm confusing and frustrating. Conversely, neurotypical individuals might misinterpret your directness as bluntness or lack empathy. Recognizing these differences is crucial. It's not about assigning blame but understanding that different people map out their emotional worlds differently.

Now, here are the golden strategies for resolving conflicts. The first is de-escalation. This is your emergency brake when emotions start running high. Techniques like taking deep breaths, asking for a pause in the conversation, or even using a pre-agreed upon safe word that signals things are getting too heated can help dial down the intensity. Another powerful tool is structured communication. This involves using clear, unambiguous language and confirming understanding as you go along. For instance, after expressing your thoughts, you might ask, "Can you share what you understood from what I just said?" This ensures you're on the same page and helps clarify any miscommunications before they escalate.

When conflicts do arise, they're not just roadblocks; they can be valuable learning experiences. Each conflict allows you to understand more about how others see things and how you react under stress. Reflecting on a disagreement can help you identify triggers that escalate conflicts, such as particular words, tones, or topics. This isn't about stewing over what went wrong but learning from the experience to handle future interactions better. Think of it as gathering intel for your growth mission, making you wiser and more prepared for the next round.

Preventive measures are not just a strategy; they are your power to set the stage for smoother interactions. Proactive communication is your tool to share your needs with others before conflict arises, giving them a map to avoid the landmines. For instance, if sudden plan changes throw you off, let your friends or colleagues know that a heads-up can help you adjust better. Clear agreements are not just rules; they are your shield, your mutual understanding that you agree on when things are calm, including handling disagreements when they arise or daily interactions that might be potential stress points. This understanding is not just crucial; it's empowering—knowing what sets off others and sharing what can upset you. It's about creating a mutual understanding that respects and protects everyone's emotional space.

Navigating conflicts as an individual on the spectrum is not just about understanding, strategy, and self-reflection. It's about turning potential battlegrounds into classrooms where everyone learns more about each other and themselves. So next time you see a conflict brewing on the horizon, remember, it's not just a challenge; it's an opportunity in disguise, ready to teach you a few things. With the right attitude, you can turn conflicts from feared encounters into moments of connection and growth, making your relational world a bit friendlier, one resolved disagreement at a time.

THE ROLE OF EMPATHY IN STRENGTHENING BONDS

What exactly is empathy? Empathy is often seen as the magic glue in relationships; it is about stepping into someone else's shoes, feeling their joys and pinches, and seeing the world from their balcony. It's a vital skill, especially in a society that sings praises of individual achievement. For those of us on the autism spectrum, empathy is sometimes a misunderstood concept. There's this myth that autistic individuals lack empathy—that we're as emotionless as a robot making morning coffee. But let me tell you, we don't lack emotion; we often experience it differently, or sometimes, even more intensely than neurotypical people.

Building empathy, therefore, isn't flipping a switch to suddenly "feel" more. It's developing the skills to understand and share the feelings of others. Let's start with perspective-taking. It consists of trying to think from another person's point of view, understanding their thoughts, and why they might feel a certain way. A simple exercise to enhance this is the "Why Game." When someone acts in a way that puzzles you, ask yourself "why" they might have behaved that way, layering each answer with another "why." This broadens your understanding and deepens your curiosity about human behavior, a key ingredient in the empathy recipe.

Next up is emotional mirroring, which about reflecting emotions you observe in others. This can be practiced through role-playing with a friend or even in front of a mirror. Try to mimic facial expressions, tone of voice, and body language. This exercise helps you connect physical expressions with emotional states, making reading emotions in real-time interactions easier. Think of it as tuning your instrument in the orchestra of social exchange, where harmony depends on every musician understanding the tune they're playing.

Increasing your level of empathy also involves a healthy dose of self-compassion and recognizing that understanding others starts with understanding yourself. Be kind to yourself when social interactions don't go as planned or when emotional cues seem as decipherable as ancient hieroglyphs. Self-compassion means permitting yourself to learn at your own pace, to make mistakes, and to recognize your growth. Celebrate the small victories, like when you understand a friend's unspoken need or share a moment of genuine connection. Remember, empathy is not just a skill; it's a journey, and you're on the right path.

Empathy, with a sprinkle of self-compassion, can significantly enhance your relationships, making them more prosperous and rewarding. It turns everyday interactions into opportunities for connection and understanding, and isn't that what we all seek? A little less judgment, a little more understanding, and many shared smiles. So, wear your empathy proudly, use it generously, and watch as it transforms your relationships and how you view the world around you.

As we close this chapter on empathy and its transformative power in relationships, reflect on how these skills can improve your connections and engage with the world. Empathy and self-compassion are not just tools for social survival; they are conduits for deeper human connection and understanding, elements that enrich our lives and the lives of those around us. As we turn the page, remember the strength in understanding others and yourself, and carry the lessons learned into the following chapters of your life.

EMPLOYMENT AND PROFESSIONAL LIFE

Whether you've been around the corporate block or are just setting foot on the career path, understanding how to navigate this maze with your sensory and cognitive needs in mind is not just a plus—it's a must. Think of this as your cheat sheet to carve out a career that excites and fulfills you.

CHOOSING THE RIGHT CAREER PATH FOR YOUR SENSORY NEEDS

Identifying Sensory-Friendly Industries

First, let's talk about the environment. Like a cactus thrives in the desert but flounders in a swamp, choosing the proper environment is crucial for your professional success and well-being. Some industries naturally offer environments that might mesh well with your sensory needs. For instance, if bustling crowds and constant chatter short-circuit your wiring, the high-energy world of stock trading might not be for you. Instead, consider paths like graphic design, IT, archival work, or research roles, often allowing for quieter spaces and more solitary work.

But it's not just about avoiding sensory overload; it's about finding sensory compatibility. Love the hum of a busy cafe? Maybe a hospitality or event management career could harness that energy in a way that feels invigorating rather than exhausting. It would be best if you matched your sensory preferences with the sensory demands of the industry.

Assessing Personal Strengths and Interests

Now, let's shine a spotlight on you. Assessing your strengths and interests doesn't mean patting yourself on the back; it means painting a picture of your professional persona. Are you great with numbers or the latest technology? Maybe detail-oriented tasks bring you joy, or does solving complex problems do it for you? Aligning your job role with what lights your fire is crucial not just for job satisfaction but for excelling in your career.

Take a moment to jot down what you're good at and what you enjoy. Sometimes, these overlap—like enjoying riddles and excelling in problem-solving. Other times, they might not come together—like enjoying social media but excelling in analytical tasks. The sweet spot? Where they intersect. And remember, this isn't set in stone. People change, interests evolve, and skills can be honed. The goal is to start with a clear map and be open to rerouting as you grow.

Case Studies of Successful Placements

Let's bring in some real-world inspirations. Zoe is a vibrant soul with a knack for numbers and a need for low sensory stimulation. She found her niche in data analysis, mainly working independently in a quiet, softly lit office. Then there's Jay, whose love for detailed craftsmanship and minimal social interaction led him to a thriving career in watchmaking. These stories underscore that understanding your sensory and cognitive needs can help you carve out a career that feels cut from the same cloth as your personality.

Guidance on Professional Assessments

If you're sitting there thinking, "But how do I figure out the right path?" professional career assessments might be your GPS. These tools help map your skills, preferences, and ideal work environments. Consider consulting a career counselor who can provide assessments like the Myers-Briggs Type Indicator or the Strong Interest Inventory. These assessments peel back layers of your professional persona, revealing paths you might not have considered.

When choosing a career counselor, look for someone with experience working with individuals with autism. They can offer insights and adjustments to the assessment process to accommodate your unique perspective. It's like having a guide who speaks your language and reads your map, helping you navigate the terrain of career planning with sensitivity to your individual traits.

Navigating the professional landscape is less about fitting into the mold and more about creating one that fits you. It's finding environments where your sensory needs aren't just accommodated but embraced as part of you. With the right understanding of what ignites your passion and how you can leverage your strengths, the world of work becomes more than accessible—it becomes your playground. So, let's roll up those sleeves and sketch a career path that celebrates every shade of your professional palette.

JOB HUNTING TIPS

Where should we begin when discussing job hunting? It's like trying to catch a unicorn in a field full of horses. It's not just about snagging any job; it's about finding the right fit—a place where your unique talents can shine and your sensory preferences aren't bombarded. Let's start with the basics—crafting a resume and cover letter that tick the boxes and highlight your extraordinary perspective.

When it comes to resumes and cover letters, think of them as your marketing brochures. They need to sing your praises, sure, but in an authentic way that highlights your unique strengths. Start by really homing in on what makes you different. Maybe it's your exceptional attention to detail, your ability to hyper-focus, or your fresh angle on problem-solving. These are real assets in the right roles. Use clear, confident language to describe these traits. For instance, instead of saying, "I'm good at details," amp it up to, "My keen attention to detail ensures high accuracy in data management." Specifics like these grab attention and paint a vivid picture of your capabilities.

Now, on to the job search itself. The internet is full of job platforms, but let's steer toward more autism-friendly ones. Websites like TheSpectrumCareers.com cater specifically to job seekers on the spectrum, offering a range of positions that value diversity in cognitive styles and work environments. Another smart move is tapping into organizations that advocate for individuals with autism. Many have job boards or partnerships with companies eager to hire diversely. These channels can often lead to opportunities with a supportive framework, making a smoother transition into a new role.

Navigating the application process can sometimes feel like decoding a secret language. From perplexing application forms to the enigma of applicant tracking systems (ATS), it is designed to filter out the uninitiated. Be sure to tailor your resume with keywords from the job description. ATS algorithms love this. They're scanning for these keywords, so sprinkle them throughout your resume like magic dust. It makes you more visible in the digital crowd. To follow up, a simple email or phone call a week after applying can show your enthusiasm without being pushy. It's like gently nudging the door to peek inside rather than knocking it down.

Leveraging your autism as a strength in your applications can set you apart. Frame it as a professional advantage. For example, if you have a knack for immersive focus, frame this as an ability to engage deeply with complex projects, highly prized in fields like software development, research, or content creation. If you're a visual thinker, highlight how this allows you to approach problems from unique angles, sparking creative solutions that might elude others. When you discuss your autism, focus on how it benefits your work, turning what some might see as a challenge into a compelling asset.

Navigating the job market as an autistic adult isn't just about finding a place to work. It's about discovering a space where your unique viewing of the world is seen as an asset, not an anomaly. You can match your unique skills with an environment that will appreciate them and thrive because of them. With tailored resumes, the right job resources, strategic application tactics, and a perspective that values your autism as a strength, you're on your way to finding the right job.

SUCCESSFUL JOB INTERVIEW TECHNIQUES

A job interview is the ultimate test of your ability to sell yourself while trying to appear calm, cool, and collected. For those of us on the autism spectrum, interviews can often feel like stepping onto a stage with all the lights suddenly glaring down. You can survive these auditions and shine with the right preparation and strategies.

Let's start with the prep work. Thoroughly researching the company is your first step. Dive into their website, check out recent news articles, and don't forget to check platforms like Glassdoor, where you can get the inside scoop from current and former employees. Understanding the company's culture, values, and recent achievements can give you topics to weave into your answers, showing them you've done your homework and are genuinely interested in being part of their team. Also, it is crucial to anticipate the questions they might ask and practice your answers. Questions like "What are your strengths?" or "Where do you see yourself in five years?" shouldn't catch you off-guard. Craft your responses to highlight your unique strengths, such as your attention to detail or ability to focus intensely on complex tasks. Make these rehearsals as real as possible; practice out loud, standing up, in the outfit you'd wear to the interview. It's all about making the actual interview feel like just another run-through.

Managing sensory issues during interviews is another critical piece of the puzzle. Consider requesting accommodations beforehand if things like fluorescent lighting or background noise throw you off. Most companies are willing to make reasonable adjustments once they understand your needs. It might be as simple as having the interview in a quieter room or turning off the overhead lights. Remember, asking for accommodations is not a sign of weakness; it ensures you can showcase your best self.

Mock interviews can be a game-changer, especially with someone who understands the specific challenges autism can bring. Whether it's a career counselor, a mentor, or even a supportive friend, practicing with someone who can provide constructive, tailored feedback can help smooth out any rough edges in your delivery. They can point out if you're speaking too fast, not making enough eye contact, or using too many filler words.

Finally, communicating your needs and abilities effectively during the interview is crucial. Be clear and concise about what you bring and how your autism is a part of that. For example, you might explain how being on the autism spectrum gives you the ability to focus intensely and manage details that others might overlook, which is a fantastic asset in roles that require precision and meticulousness. Also, be upfront about the accommodations you need to perform your best. Framing these needs as part of your unique approach to work can help potential employers see them not as obstacles but as aspects of your distinctive strengths.

You're well-equipped for any interview with thorough preparation, strategies to manage sensory issues, practice through mock interviews, and clear communication about your needs and strengths. So, take a deep breath, gather your notes, and get ready to show the world—or at least the interview panel—what makes you an outstanding candidate. Remember, it's not just about getting the job; it's about finding a place to contribute, prosper, and grow.

ADVOCATING FOR WORKPLACE ACCOMMODATIONS

Workplace accommodations can transform your work environment from a daily grind into a place where you can genuinely shine. Before you start envisioning elaborate modifications, let's get grounded with the basics—the legal rights under laws like the Americans with Disabilities Act (ADA). This legislation ensures you have the right to request modifications that enable you to perform your job without undue hardship. Understanding this law isn't just bureaucratic hoop-jumping—it empowers you to advocate for an environment tailored to your unique needs.

Effectively communicating your needs isn't just about what you say. It's about how you frame it. Approach the conversation with confidence and clarity, focusing on how accommodations can enhance your productivity and, by extension, benefit the team. It's about mutual gains as much as personal comfort. For instance, if you thrive in a quieter environment, explain how this change could enhance your concentration, leading to faster turnaround times or fewer errors in your work. It's like pitching a new idea to your boss; you want to highlight the benefits, not just the features.

Let's dive into some standard accommodations that might ring true for you. Alternative lighting, for instance, can be a game-changer if harsh fluorescent lights make your sensory alarms go off. Requesting softer, natural light options not only eases your sensory overload but can also create a more calming atmosphere, boosting overall productivity. Then there's flexible scheduling— perhaps starting later when you're more alert or working from home during particularly demanding projects. These adjustments don't just make your day-to-day easier; they optimize your performance.

Documenting these accommodations is your safety net. It ensures that you and your employer understand the agreed-upon changes and their intended outcomes. This can be as simple as a follow-up email after a discussion outlining what was agreed upon and the next steps. Keeping a record ensures clarity and accountability. It's like maintaining receipts; they're not just paper trails but proof of your proactive approach to navigating your professional landscape.

Handling the request for accommodations can sometimes feel like you're asking for special treatment, but remember, it's about leveling the playing field, not getting an unfair advantage. With a solid understanding of your legal rights, a strategic approach to communication, practical examples of possible adjustments, and a good system for documenting everything, you're well-equipped to advocate for a work environment that recognizes and celebrates your unique way of interacting with the world. So, arm yourself with knowledge, prepare your pitch, and remember, you're paving the way for a more inclusive and productive workplace.

NETWORKING STRATEGIES FOR INTROVERTED ADULTS

The word "Networking" can send shivers down the spine of any self-respecting introvert. It conjures up images of schmoozing at cocktail parties or shouting over loud music at crowded bars, all in the name of making professional connections. But what if I told you that networking doesn't have to be a nightmare? There are ways to network that can feel pretty cozy for introverts, with genuine connections being made. Let's explore introvert-friendly strategies to build your professional network without draining your social battery.

First, let's talk about online networking. It's like the introvert's secret weapon. Platforms like LinkedIn are goldmines for making connections without the awkwardness of face-to-face interactions. Start by sprucing up your profile. Think of it as your digital handshake—firm, confident, and friendly. Highlight your unique skills and experiences, and don't shy away from mentioning your work style and strengths, especially those that resonate with being on the autism spectrum. These details can attract like-minded professionals and open doors to opportunities that value your talents and work approach. Engage with content relevant to your field by leaving thoughtful comments or sharing interesting articles. This allows you to start conversations in a space where you feel comfortable, at your own pace, one click at a time.

If the idea of significant networking events makes you want to run for the hills, consider smaller, more intimate meetups or one-on-one meetings. Many professional groups host smaller gatherings where you can engage more deeply with a few people at a time. These settings are often less intimidating and allow for more meaningful exchanges that can lead to stronger, more personal connections. It's like having a mini power session where you can talk shop, exchange ideas, and build relationships that feel less like passing acquaintances and more like professional allies. And if small meetups are still too much, why not try reaching out for coffee meetings? A quiet chat with coffee and two professionals can sometimes prove more fruitful than any big-ticket networking event.

Building relationships gradually is critical. Rome wasn't built in a day, nor is a robust professional network. It's okay to take your time to nurture connections. Follow up a LinkedIn conversation with an email, or send a note expressing your pleasure in discussing shared interests after a meetup. Regular, low-pressure interactions help build familiarity and trust, paving the way for a network that grows organically. Lay one brick at a time, ensuring each fits perfectly before adding the next.

Finally, remember that in networking, quality tops quantity every time. Quality connections are more likely to be supportive, engage more deeply with your professional development, and provide more significant opportunities. A network built on mutual respect and genuine interaction is not just a career asset; it's a treasure trove of resources, inspiration, and support.

Well, there you have it—a guide to networking that even the most introverted can navigate comfortably. Start online, choose smaller gatherings, build connections gradually, and focus on quality over quantity. With these strategies, you'll find that building a professional network doesn't have to be overwhelming or exhausting. Instead, it can be a rewarding extension of your professional life, filled with connections that advance and enrich your career. So, take a deep breath, set your own pace, and start building a network that works not just for your career but also for you.

MANAGING PROFESSIONAL RELATIONSHIPS AND AUTISM

Navigating the professional waters can sometimes feel like you're piloting a submarine—lots of buttons and levers, and you've got to keep an eye on everything to avoid a crash. Now, sprinkle in the complexities of autism, and it's like you're managing that submarine through an underwater cave, lit only by your understanding of your needs and how you communicate them. Let's set the stage for smoothing this journey, focusing on setting clear expectations, handling misunderstandings, crafting effective feedback loops, and championing self-advocacy.

Setting clear expectations from the start is like laying down the rules of a board game before you begin playing—it makes everything smoother. When you're upfront with your colleagues and supervisors about how you work best, it demystifies your processes and sets a clear pathway for collaboration. For instance, if direct emails with bullet-pointed tasks work better for you than impromptu desk chats, make that known. It's also helpful to clarify how you handle social interactions in the workplace. Maybe large group meetings are taxing for you, and you perform better in smaller, focused discussions. Communicating this prevents misinterpretations of your work style, such as disinterest or non-engagement. You're crafting a work environment set up for success from day one.

Dealing with misunderstandings requires strategies, especially when differences in communication styles come into play. Misunderstandings can escalate quickly when you perceive information through your unique lens. For example, a casually thrown "Can you handle this?" might feel like an accusation to you, while it was intended as a genuine question by a colleague. To navigate these tricky waters, develop a habit of seeking clarification before reacting. A simple "Could you explain what you mean by that?" can open a dialogue that helps clear the air and deepen mutual understanding. Also, having a trusted ally at work who understands your communication style can help bridge gaps. This ally can mediate or clarify situations where there might be a disconnect between your intentions and how others perceive them.

Establishing regular feedback loops with supervisors and peers is essential. These checks ensure everything runs smoothly and any minor issues can be addressed before becoming more significant problems. Encourage a culture of open, ongoing communication by scheduling regular one-on-one meetings with your supervisor, where you can discuss your progress, challenges, and strategies for improvement. Similarly, periodic check-ins with peers can foster a team environment that values transparency and support. These feedback sessions are invaluable for adjusting your work approach and refining how you interact with your team.

Self-advocacy in the workplace is your power tool. It means confidently voicing your needs and the unique perspectives you bring to the table. People on the spectrum often bring a level of detail-oriented focus and innovative problem-solving skills that can be a tremendous asset in many professional settings. However, these skills can only be fully utilized if the work environment accommodates your way of processing and responding to information. Advocate for yourself by highlighting how specific accommodations or adjustments can lead to better outcomes for you, the team, and the company. Whether requesting particular tools or software, adjustments in workflow, or even the way information is communicated, every modification that helps you perform better is a testament to the company's commitment to diversity and inclusion.

Navigating professional relationships isn't just about adapting; it's about creating a work environment that recognizes and leverages your unique traits. From setting clear expectations and managing misunderstandings to establishing effective feedback mechanisms and advocating for your needs, these strategies make your job easier and enrich your professional life, ensuring you're fully engaged and appreciated for your unique strengths.

In wrapping up this chapter, remember that each strategy you employ is a step toward a more fulfilling professional experience. Whether it's through setting clear expectations, handling misunderstandings with grace, or advocating for conditions that allow you to thrive, each action you take builds a stronger foundation for your career. As we move forward, these principles enhance your professional interactions and empower you to navigate the broader aspects of your life with confidence and clarity. Next, we'll explore daily living skills and independence, diving into practical tips and strategies to manage everyday tasks and responsibilities.

DAILY LIVING SKILLS AND INDEPENDENCE

I magine this: it's payday, and your bank account got a lovely boost. You feel ready to conquer the world—or at least the supermarket. But then, the anxiety sets in. Bills to pay, savings to stash away, are you saving enough for that rainy day everyone talks about? Fear not! This chapter is your guide to navigating the choppy waters of financial management with flair, breaking down everything from budget basics to taming the anxiety monster that often accompanies money matters.

FINANCIAL PLANNING AND MANAGEMENT

Understanding Financial Basics

Let's start with the ABCs of finance—budgeting, saving, and the importance of planning. Think of a budget as your financial roadmap; it shows you where your money is coming from, where it's going, and where you can save. The first step is simple: track your income and your expenses. Those coffee runs and online purchases add up quickly. Once you have a clear picture of everything, categorize your expenses into "needs" (like rent and groceries) and "wants" (like that latest tech gadget or designer jacket). This helps create a budget that keeps your finances in check and allows room for the occasional splurge.

Saving is next on the list. It's like preparing for a financial storm—it might not be fun to think about, but it brings peace of mind. Start small. Even a tiny portion of your paycheck stashed away each month can grow into a substantial safety net. The key here is consistency. Treat your savings like a bill that must be paid every month. Over time, this disciplined approach can help you build a cushion that protects you from unexpected expenses or financial emergencies.

Tools for Financial Management

Now, let's make things interesting with some tech talk. In this digital age, managing your finances can be as easy as tapping on your smartphone. Apps and tools designed for budgeting and financial tracking can be lifesavers, especially for those who find numbers daunting. Apps like Mint or YNAB (You Need A Budget) link with your bank accounts to help you track spending in real-time, categorize expenses, and even set budgets that alert you when you're close to the limit. These tools can be beneficial in maintaining a routine and reducing the cognitive load associated with financial management.

Dealing with Financial Anxiety

Let's tackle the elephant in the room—financial anxiety. It's like that annoying relative who shows up uninvited to every family gathering. First, recognize that it's okay to feel anxious. Money is a big deal, after all. But here's how to keep those nerves under wraps: automate what you can. Set up automatic transfers to your savings account, automate bill payments, and use reminders for due dates. Automation is like putting your financial responsibilities on autopilot so you can relax knowing that the essentials are covered.

Seeking Professional Help

Sometimes, despite our best efforts, the world of finance can still be overwhelming. When there are complicated issues to consider, such as investments, large purchases, or planning for retirement— it's perfectly okay to call in a professional. Financial advisors are a great reference to use on your financial journey. They help map out the best routes and ensure you avoid potholes. Look for advisors who have experience working with clients on the autism spectrum or are known for their patient and clear communication style. Don't hesitate to ask all the questions you need—after all, it's your money, and you have the right to know where it's going and why.

With these strategies, you can manage your money with confidence and minimal stress. Remember, financial independence isn't just about having wealth; it's about having control over your finances in a way that brings peace of mind and security, letting you enjoy the fruits of your labor without the constant worry. So, take charge of your financial journey with the tips shared here, and watch your confidence and bank balance grow.

ORGANIZATIONAL SKILLS TO COMBAT EXECUTIVE DYSFUNCTION

Executive dysfunction is a familiar, unwelcome guest in the lives of many adults with autism. It's like trying to juggle while riding a unicycle uphill. Executive dysfunction can smear your day with forgetfulness, distractibility, and pervasive disarray.

First, let's decode executive dysfunction. In adults with autism, this often means difficulties with planning, memory, task initiation, and shifting between tasks. It's not just about being a little forgetful or disorganized; your brain manages its cognitive resources in a way that makes traditional organizational strategies about as effective as using a sieve to scoop water. Recognizing this is key—it's not a flaw in your character. A particular wiring in your brain needs a different approach to manage this effectively.

Let's talk about planners, apps, and visual cues. Apps are great to use for your organizational advantage. Apps like Trello or Asana can help you visualize tasks as cards that move from one column to another, mimicking a physical movement that can be particularly satisfying. For a more in-your-face approach, try reminder apps that send you nudging notifications for everything from taking medication to paying bills. Set them up with quirky alarms that remind you and make you smile. Remember, the goal is to make these tools an extension of your mind, helping you navigate tasks with fewer hiccups.

But maybe digital isn't your thing, or perhaps you prefer a blend of old-school and new-tech methods. Enter the hybrid approach—using both physical planners and digital tools. Start with a large wall planner—a visual feast of your month at a glance. Color-code tasks—green for go, red for stop and reassess, yellow for caution or pending tasks. Complement this with your digital tools for on-the-go tracking. This method bridges the tactile satisfaction of writing things down with the convenience and mobility of digital apps. I can personally attest to the effectiveness of this method. I have a large desk calendar that I scribble on daily, but I also use several apps on my phone.

Customizing these systems is like tailoring a suit. It needs to fit your life's rhythms and routines snugly. If you're a visual thinker, make your tools colorful and image-rich. Set up detailed lists and spreadsheets if you'd like. The key is consistency and personalization. Make your organizational methods so seamlessly integrated into your daily life that not using them feels like stepping out without your shoes. Adjust and tweak them as your routines change. What works today might need a revision next month or next year. Stay flexible, and keep refining your system.

Also, consider the everyday hurdles of procrastination and maintaining motivation. Procrastination is often more about anxiety or unclear instructions than laziness or poor time management. Tackle this by breaking tasks into micro-tasks. Instead of "clean the house," break it down: organize books on the shelf, vacuum the living room, and wipe down kitchen counters. Suddenly, what seemed overwhelming was just a series of small, manageable tasks. As for motivation, find what sparks your enthusiasm. Maybe it's rewarding yourself with a favorite snack or an episode of your favorite show after completing a task. Or perhaps it's setting up a mini celebration for the weekend if you tick off all your tasks for the week. Make it fun and rewarding, and watch your motivation soar.

Managing executive dysfunction is about understanding how your brain functions and outfitting yourself with the strategies that align with your needs. Equip yourself with these steps, adapt them, and prepare to tackle your tasks with a newfound sense of control and confidence.

NAVIGATING PUBLIC TRANSPORTATION AND TRAVEL

Thinking ahead is ideal when traveling, especially when using public transportation. Start by becoming a mini expert on your travel route. Dive into researching bus schedules, train timings, or subway maps. Apps like Google Maps or Citymapper can be lifesavers here, giving you real-time updates and step-by-step navigation. But don't just stop at knowing the route—get familiar with the transit stops, the environment around them, and alternative routes in case of unexpected changes. This kind of preparation not only eases your mind but also arms you with the confidence to handle the uncertainties of travel.

Now, let's add some additional tech to your travel plans. Technology today has made traveling significantly less daunting. Real-time transit updates can alert you to delays or cancellations, allowing you to adjust your plans. GPS apps are like having a compass that guides you in the right direction and informs you of the terrain ahead. For those who treasure predictability and routine, these apps are like a trusted travel companion who whispers, "Hey, so that you know, there's a 10-minute delay on your usual route. Maybe grab a coffee while you wait?" Also, consider travel planning tools that offer accessibility features, providing information like elevator availability for those with mobility issues or quiet car options for those who might get overwhelmed by noise.

Handling sensory challenges while on the go is crucial. Public transportation can overwhelm the senses of even a neurotypical traveler—honking buses, screeching trains, and crowds that buzz like a hive of bees. To keep sensory overload at bay, pay attention to timing. Travel during off-peak hours when fewer people are around. This could mean leaving earlier for your appointment or waiting out the peak rush. Equip yourself with noise-canceling headphones to mute the chaos, sunglasses to dim overly bright lights, or tactile objects like a stress ball to squeeze when anxiety levels rise.

Building confidence in using public transportation doesn't happen overnight. It's like building muscle; the more you use it, the stronger it gets. Start with shorter trips that aren't far from your comfort zone. Maybe it's a quick ride to a familiar cafe or a brief excursion to a local library. Bring a friend or family member who understands your needs and can offer support if things get tricky. Each successful trip adds a layer of confidence, slowly stretching the boundaries of your comfort zone. Over time, what once felt like an insurmountable challenge will start to feel like just another part of your day.

Navigating public transportation can be a challenging journey. Still, proper preparation, tools, and strategies can also lead to greater independence and confidence. By researching routes, leveraging technology, managing sensory challenges, and gradually increasing your exposure to travel, you transform public transportation from a source of stress to a gateway to new experiences. The world is waiting, and you're ready to navigate it on your terms.

COOKING AND MEAL PREPARATION: SIMPLIFIED STRATEGIES

OK, now let's focus on cooking! You're not alone if the kitchen feels more like a battlefield than a chef's paradise. Many adults, particularly those of us on the autism spectrum, find cooking to range from mildly intimidating to downright chaotic. But with a few clever strategies and creativity, you can transform your kitchen from a place of stress to a peaceful haven.

Mastering basic cooking skills can set you up for culinary independence. Start simple. I'm talking about basic skills like boiling pasta, scrambling eggs, or making a simple salad. These aren't just recipes; they're your building blocks to more complex dishes. Once the basics are down, you can mix and match these skills to create new creations. For instance, once you conquer the art of boiling pasta, a whole world of pasta-based dishes awaits— add some sautéed veggies, a protein of your choice, and voilà, you've got a meal. And remember, cooking should be fun! Play your favorite music and maybe dance around a little as you chop and stir—it's about making the kitchen joyful.

Meal planning and grocery shopping are next on the menu. Planning your meals for the week might seem like a chore, but it's a game-changer for reducing stress and avoiding that mid-week meal panic. Start by jotting down a few meal ideas and the necessary ingredients. Keep it flexible; maybe plan for five meals and leave a few nights for leftovers or takeout. Now, grocery shopping—this can be a sensory overload minefield. Bright lights, crowded aisles, and a cacophony of sounds can seem like a lot. Here's a tip: try online grocery shopping. It's a fantastic way to manage sensory challenges while getting your needs. You can browse at your own pace, and it's all delivered right to your door.

If online isn't an option, consider going during off-peak hours or making a precise list to make the trip quicker and less stressful, or choose curbside delivery at the grocery store if you have your own vehicle (or someone to go with you).

Let's talk about making your kitchen more autism friendly. Organizing your cooking space can significantly reduce stress. Group items by use—for instance, keep all your baking ingredients together or have a specific spot for spices. This saves time and minimizes the frustration of searching through cabinets. Also, consider the sensory aspects of your kitchen. If the fluorescent lights are too harsh, switch them out for softer, warmer bulbs. If the noise from the kitchen appliances is too much, look for quieter alternatives while you cook.

Safety in the kitchen is crucial. It's easy to get overwhelmed by the heat, the sharp knives, and the multitasking. Always keep a fire extinguisher accessible—better safe than sorry. When it comes to knives, invest in a good set and keep them sharp; a sharp knife is safer as it requires less force to cut through food. Learn to turn pot handles away from the front of the stove to avoid accidental spills. And here's a safety plus—always have a routine for checking that everything is turned off before you leave the kitchen. Maybe do a final walk-through or keep a checklist on the fridge. You want to create a safe space where the only thing you need to worry about is whether to add more garlic to your dish.

By implementing these strategies, cooking can transform from a daunting task to an enjoyable and nourishing part of your day. It's not just about feeding yourself; it's about crafting a space where you feel confident and in control, respecting your sensory needs, and celebrating your independence.

HOME ORGANIZATION FOR SENSORY AND PRACTICAL EFFICIENCY

Home should be a sanctuary where you can kick off your shoes, unwind, and be yourself. For those of us with autism, creating a living space that minimizes sensory overstimulation isn't just about comfort; it's about survival. So, let's transform your living space into a sensory-friendly place where calmness rules.

Lighting can make or break your comfort in a space. Those harsh fluorescent bulbs that make your living room feel like an interrogation room? Swap them out for softer, warmer LED lights that mimic natural sunlight, offering a gentler touch on your sensory system. If natural light is an option, embrace it. Natural light can significantly uplift your mood and reduce the harshness often associated with artificial lighting. Noise control is another biggie. Thick curtains or even specialized soundproofing panels can be a game-changer if you're sensitive to external noises. These adjustments don't require a significant overhaul—a few tweaks here and there can turn a nerve-racking space into a soothing spot.

Now, let's chat about decluttering. Clutter is more than an aesthetic issue; it's a sensory and mental load that can feel overwhelming. Start by decluttering in waves. It's less daunting that way. Begin with one room or part of a room—maybe your desk or a particular drawer. The key is to create designated spots for your belongings. Use labels if it helps. This eases your visual landscape and saves you the sensory and mental hassle of sifting through piles of stuff to find what you need. The less clutter, the less cleaning, and who isn't a fan of that?

Speaking of cleaning, let's roll up our sleeves and dive into some strategies to keep your home neat without turning it into a full-time job. Routine is your ally here. Break down your cleaning tasks into a schedule—dusting on Tuesdays, vacuuming on Thursdays, etc. Make cleaning predictable and manageable. Consider using checklists or apps to track what's done and pending. This keeps you organized and visually represents your progress, which can be incredibly satisfying. For those days when motivation is low, focus on micro-tasks. Don't think about cleaning the whole house; focus on organizing your bookshelf or cleaning the kitchen counter. Small victories can lead to big rewards in maintaining order and cleanliness.

Finally, let's personalize your space. Your home should reflect your tastes, your needs, and your comforts. If certain textures soothe you, incorporate them into your decor—think soft throw pillows, velvet curtains, or a plush rug. Colors also play a significant role in sensory processing. Maybe calming blues and greens work best for you, or perhaps you prefer the energizing hues of yellows and oranges. Use these to create a space that looks and feels good. Personalization also means making functional adjustments that cater to your unique needs. If certain furniture arrangements or setups work better for your sensory preferences or mobility needs, don't hesitate to make those changes. Your home is your realm; customize it to be where every corner, every color, and every cushion lets you feel at ease, in control, and genuinely at home.

Creating a sensory-friendly and efficiently organized home is about crafting a space that supports your sensory needs, simplifies your routines, and reflects your style. You can turn your living environment into a shelter that supports your senses and emotions.

PERSONAL SAFETY AND EMERGENCY PREPAREDNESS

Feeling safe and prepared is essential for our mental and physical well-being. We will discuss the knowledge and skills needed to confidently protect yourself and navigate emergencies.

Understanding Personal Safety

Personal safety starts with a solid awareness of your environment. Start by familiarizing yourself with your regular haunts—know the exits in your favorite cafe, the quiet corners in your local library, and the busiest times at your grocery store. This isn't about paranoia; it's about preparedness. Basic self-defense skills can also boost your confidence. Many communities offer classes tailored to different abilities and needs, providing simple techniques to help you feel more secure. Remember, the goal isn't to become a martial arts expert; it's to give you a sense of control over your personal space and safety.

Emergency Preparedness

Next up, let's tackle emergency preparedness. Think of an emergency kit as your go-to for unexpected adventures—ones you'd rather not have. This kit should include basics like water, non-perishable food, a flashlight, batteries, a first aid kit, and essential medications. But let's personalize it to cater to your needs and requirements. If routine is crucial for mental stability, include a written schedule or familiar items to help you in stressful situations. Store this kit in an easily accessible place, and do a run-through every few months to replace expired items and update it as your needs change. Planning for emergencies might sound daunting, but think of it as packing for a trip—one you hope you'll never take but for which you're thoroughly prepared.

De-escalation Techniques

Dealing with confrontations or high-stress situations requires a cool head and a set of de-escalation techniques. These are ways to defuse a situation before it escalates. Start with your body language: maintain an open posture and avoid direct eye contact, which can be perceived as challenging. Use a calm, low tone of voice, and listen actively. Sometimes, people want to be heard. Offer simple options to resolve the conflict and know when to walk away. It's about managing the situation, not winning an argument. Practice these techniques in lower-stress environments so that if you ever need to use them, they come as naturally as breathing.

Resources for Further Learning

Finally, keep your safety skills sharp by tapping into further learning resources. Many communities offer classes in personal safety and emergency preparedness. These can be great opportunities to learn new skills and connect with others looking to boost their safety know-how. Online tutorials can also be valuable, especially if attending in-person classes feels overwhelming. Websites like the Red Cross offer free resources on everything from basic first aid to detailed emergency preparedness plans.

Navigating the world with an awareness of personal safety and emergency preparedness enhances your independence. It gives you the confidence to handle whatever life brings. So, equip yourself with these skills, practice them regularly, and remember, being prepared isn't about expecting the worst; it's about being ready to meet any challenge with calmness and confidence. Now, as we close this chapter on mastering daily living skills and stepping into the world with assurance, let's carry forward this newfound confidence and readiness into the realms of social interaction and community engagement, where your safety skills and preparedness mindset will continue to serve you and amplify your ability to navigate and thrive in the wider world.

ACCESSING RESOURCES AND COMMUNITY SUPPORT

I magine you're gearing up for a grand expedition into the wild —now, swap out the wild for the world of autism communities and resources. The various support groups and online platforms are designed to make your journey less "Where am I?" and more "I've got this!" This chapter will guide you through the resources available, ensuring you find the right group of people for your optimal level of support.

IDENTIFYING HELPFUL LOCAL AND ONLINE AUTISM COMMUNITIES

Discover Local Support Groups

Embarking on the journey to find local support groups is like discovering your favorite little coffee shop, where everyone knows your order. It's a comforting and crucial part of your routine. But how do you find these hidden gems? Start with a simple online search or check out community bulletin boards at libraries or community centers. Many towns and cities have groups specifically for adults on the spectrum. Like a personal cheer squad, these groups meet regularly to share experiences, exchange coping strategies, and foster friendships. They understand the quirks and qualms of being on the autism spectrum, making them a valuable part of your support network.

But it's not just about showing up; it's about finding the right fit. Think of it as trying on shoes. Some might look great but feel terrible, while others might not catch your eye until you try them on and realize they're perfect. Attend a few meetings, get a feel for the group's dynamics, and see if they match your needs. Are they more about social outings, or do they focus on educational workshops? Do you prefer a group with deep discussions, or are you looking for a lighter touch? Finding the right group is crucial because the proper support can make all the difference in enhancing your journey through the spectrum.

Benefits of Online Communities

Now, let's explore the digital landscape. Online communities, such as forums and Facebook groups, are like the international airports of the autism world. They connect you to people from all walks of life, anywhere in the world, all from the comfort of your home. These platforms offer anonymity and accessibility, making them a great option if you're geographically isolated or if stepping into a room of strangers is impossible. You can share your story, ask for advice, or scroll through and read about others' experiences. You connect on your terms, in your own time, making these communities a flexible and convenient part of your support system.

As you venture into these online communities, it's crucial to gauge the group's dynamics. Is it a lively hub of activity or a deserted ghost town? Are trolls swiftly dealt with, or is it a free-for-all? The tone and supportiveness of the group are vital factors to consider. You want to be part of a community that uplifts its members, fostering a positive and supportive environment.

Community Engagement Checklist

- **Introduce yourself.** Give a brief, honest introduction.
- **Participate actively.** Ask questions and share experiences.
- **Respect norms.** Understand and follow group rules.
- **Give and take.** Balance your contributions with active listening.
- **Put safety first.** Protect your privacy, and respect others' boundaries.

Navigating the world of autism support groups and online communities isn't just about finding a place to fit in. It's about finding a space to be yourself, learn from others, and perhaps help others along the way. You can build a network that supports you, challenges you, and cheers for you as you navigate the spectrum.

UTILIZING SOCIAL MEDIA FOR SUPPORT AND ADVOCACY

Don't underestimate the power of social media in your quest for community engagement. Navigating the bustling digital landscape can sometimes feel like you're a small fish in a vast ocean. But fear not because, with the right strategies, you can turn these platforms into powerful allies. Each social media platform has its unique flavor and audience, making it crucial to pick the right one for your needs. X (formerly Twitter), for instance, is like the bustling town square of the internet, perfect for quick, impactful messages and joining more significant conversations, especially during awareness campaigns. On the other hand, Instagram is your digital art gallery where personal stories and visual content reign supreme, making it ideal for sharing your journey and connecting on a more personal level. Facebook has many groups for autism, some general, some specific to adults. So, use these platforms to your advantage, share your experiences, and connect with others in the autism community. Your voice matters, and social media can be a powerful tool for amplifying it.

Creating impactful content is an art that starts with a clear goal. Are you aiming to educate, inspire, or advocate for change? Defining your purpose will steer your content creation. For instance, if you aim to educate, consider using infographics and detailed posts about autism and its nuances. On the other hand, sharing personal stories about your experiences can be powerful if you're looking to inspire. Remember, authenticity is critical. People can sense when you're genuine, and that fosters deeper connections and engagement. Don't forget to adjust your privacy settings to your comfort level. Social media should be a tool you control, not one that controls you. Set boundaries to ensure a safe and positive experience.

Now, let's talk about amplifying your voice by connecting with influencers and organizations within the autism community. Think of influencers as the megaphones of the digital world. When they speak, people listen. Start by identifying influencers whose values align with yours. Engage with their content thoughtfully— comment, share, and perhaps even collaborate. This increases your visibility and helps you become a part of a more extensive network that can drive change. Similarly, connecting with organizations can provide you with more platforms to share your voice, access to resources, and opportunities to participate in campaigns or events. It's about creating partnerships where your personal experiences can contribute to broader advocacy efforts.

Dealing with negativity and trolls is an unfortunate but sometimes inevitable part of the online world. The key is to refrain from engaging with them. Responding to negative comments or people looking to provoke can drain your energy and distract from your message. Know when to respond and when to let things slide. If a comment genuinely seeks understanding or a different perspective, a thoughtful response could enlighten all involved. However, if someone is there to cause trouble, your best option is to use the block and report functions. Social media platforms have policies and moderation tools designed to maintain a safe environment; don't hesitate to use them. Remember, your mental health and well-being come first. You're here to make a difference, not to win every argument.

Navigating social media as a tool for support and advocacy in the autism community involves choosing the right platforms, creating impactful content, connecting with influencers and organizations, and managing interactions carefully. By harnessing the power of these digital platforms, you can amplify your voice, reach out to those who need to hear your message and contribute to a more informed and inclusive society. So, set your sights on those digital horizons and use your unique perspective and experiences to fuel your journey in the vast, ever-expanding world of social media.

EDUCATIONAL PROGRAMS AND WORKSHOPS FOR ADULTS

So, you're thinking about hitting the books again or maybe sharpening some skills through a workshop? Venturing back into the world of learning as an adult—especially one on the autism spectrum—can feel a bit like stepping back into the gym after a prolonged break. It's a bit daunting, sure, but so rewarding. Let's explore how you can find educational programs and workshops tailored to your unique needs and why this could be one of the best decisions you can make for your personal and professional life. These programs can enhance your knowledge and skills, boost your self-confidence, and open new opportunities. So, don't hesitate to invest in your learning and development. It's a journey that's worth taking.

First off, find the right programs. This isn't just picking any class off the list; it's about finding courses that resonate with your interests and cater to your learning style. Community colleges and universities often offer continuing education courses designed for adult learners. These aren't your typical undergrad courses; they're geared toward individuals juggling a job, family responsibilities, or other adult obligations alongside their educational pursuits. Additionally, many institutions are now recognizing the need to support learners on the spectrum. This might include accommodations like providing course materials in advance, offering lecture recordings, or ensuring quiet spaces for breaks.

For something less formal but equally enriching, look for skill-building workshops or seminars. Local community centers, libraries, or even autism advocacy organizations frequently host events focused on everything from coding workshops to creative writing classes. And here's a pro tip: don't forget to check out online platforms like Coursera or Udemy. They offer many courses you can take from the comfort of your home, which is perfect if you find in-person settings challenging or your schedule is incredibly tight.

But why should you dust off the old notebook and get back to learning, you ask? Well, let's talk perks. Continuing your education can boost your self-esteem. There's something incredibly empowering about mastering a new skill or expanding your knowledge. Plus, learning new skills can expand your social network. Whether it's a classmate, a workshop peer, or even an online study group, you'll be connecting with people who share your interests. And let's not forget the potential career benefits. Adding new skills and certifications can significantly improve your resume, potentially opening doors to job opportunities that might have been out of reach.

Choosing the right program also means considering accessibility and accommodations. Before enrolling, reach out to the program coordinators. Discuss how the course is delivered, what support is available, and whether accommodations suit your needs. You must feel supported, and the environment must be conducive to your learning style. Ask about the qualifications and experience of those running the program. Instructors who are experienced in working with adults on the spectrum can make the learning experience more accessible and enjoyable. Remember, every class, every workshop, and every new bit of knowledge is a stepping stone toward a more fulfilled, more skilled, and more connected you.

LEGAL RIGHTS AND ADVOCACY FOR ADULTS WITH AUTISM

We previously discussed using the Americans with Disabilities Act (ADA) to ensure that you are treated fairly at work and to make sure that you are provided with reasonable accommodations. Advocating for yourself and others is the next step. Self-advocacy goes beyond knowing your rights and requires actively asserting them. Every significant change in society started with a few brave people. Begin by documenting instances where you feel your rights were compromised. This documentation can be a powerful tool for discussing the accommodations you need with employers, educators, or service providers. Engaging with disability rights organizations can also amplify your efforts. These groups can provide resources, support, and guidance on navigating advocacy in more structured ways, such as participating in legislative processes or public demonstrations.

Now, let's talk about navigating the legal system, which, for many, can seem as approachable as a fortress surrounded by moats. The key here is finding allies who are well-versed in disability rights law. Lawyers specializing in this area can be invaluable guides, helping you understand the nuances of your rights and the best strategies for defending them. When looking for a lawyer, seek out those with a track record of handling cases similar to yours, and don't shy away from asking about their experience and approach. A good lawyer isn't just a legal representative; they're a partner in your quest for justice.

To bring this to life, consider the case of a group of adults with autism who banded together to challenge a local government policy that indirectly discriminated against adults with disabilities in the allocation of housing resources. With the help of a skilled legal team and the support of a national disability rights organization, they not only succeeded in changing the policy but also secured additional funding for programs specifically aimed at adults with autism. This case improved conditions for the plaintiffs and set a precedent that benefited others in the community.

Navigating your legal rights and advocacy avenues can help you achieve personal empowerment and pave the way for broader change. It's about transforming obstacles into stepping stones and using your voice to echo the call for justice and equality.

FINDING AND WORKING WITH AUTISM SPECIALISTS

First, let's talk about identifying the right specialists— psychiatrists, psychologists, or occupational therapists. Start with a bit of research. Online directories of healthcare professionals can be a good starting point. Websites like Psychology Today allow you to filter your search based on specialties, treatment approaches, and even which insurance providers they accept. But be sure to look for those who specify experience with autism spectrum disorders, particularly in adults. Adult autism can present differently than childhood autism, and you'll want someone who understands the difference.

Don't stop there. Check out local and national autism organizations—they often have resources or networks that can point you to specialists experienced in adult autism. And remember, the autism community is your ally. Tap into forums, social media groups, or local community groups to ask for recommendations. Sometimes, the best leads come from those who've walked the path before you and can point you to a specialist who's made a real difference in their lives.

But how do you prep for that first appointment? Preparation is essential. Arm yourself with the main issues or concerns you want to address. Write them down so you don't forget anything important during the appointment. Bring any past medical or psychological evaluations and a list of any medications you're currently taking. This isn't just paperwork; it's your backstory, your user manual of sorts, that can give your specialist a head start in understanding your unique needs.

As you embark on your therapeutic journey, it's important to assess how comfortable you feel with your specialist. Are they listening to you with empathy? Do they explain things in a way that you understand? Are they open to discussing and integrating your input into the treatment plan? Remember, therapy is a two-way street that requires collaboration. You want someone who's not just an expert but a partner in your journey towards better mental health.

What if you feel that the specialist isn't the right fit? It's perfectly normal. As we discussed, trying out various specialists is a part of the process. If you find yourself dreading sessions or feeling that your concerns aren't being addressed, it might be time to consider switching to a different professional. This might feel like starting over, but remember, your well-being is worth the effort. When ending the therapeutic relationship, be honest and respectful. While you appreciate their efforts, you can express that a different specialist might be better suited to your needs. Then, use the insights from this experience to find someone who might be a better match.

Finding and working with the right autism specialists is crucial in managing your needs effectively. It's about finding someone who doesn't just add to your list of appointments but enriches your support system, providing you with understanding, practical strategies, and genuine progress. The right specialist is out there. With a bit of persistence, you'll find them.

GOVERNMENT AND PRIVATE FINANCIAL AID OPTIONS

Wading through the muddy waters of government and private funding options designed for adults with autism can feel like a daunting chore. With the correct information, the process can transform into a strategic mission to bolster your financial stability.

Let's start by exploring the vast landscape of financial aid available. These might include Social Security Disability Insurance (SSDI) or Medicaid waivers specifically tailored to individuals with disabilities, ensuring that basic needs are met. But the support doesn't stop there. Various scholarships and grants are also up for grabs, specifically targeting adults with autism eager to pursue further education or vocational training. These aren't just handouts; they're investments in your potential, designed to give you a leg up in achieving your personal and professional goals.

As you begin the application process, you must arm yourself with patience and a hefty dose of organization. Each form of aid, whether a government program or a private grant, comes with its rules and requirements. Start by gathering all necessary documents—medical records that confirm an autism diagnosis, proof of income, and any previous benefit records. It's like assembling your gear before a hike; having everything ready can make the journey smoother. Most applications can now be handled online, which adds a layer of convenience but also demands precision—double-check entries for accuracy to avoid delays. Remember, the bureaucracy can be slow, but persistence is vital. Keep copies of all your submissions, and don't hesitate to follow up regularly. Treat it like a job where meticulousness and persistence are your primary duties.

Now, let's explore the art of maximizing your financial resources. This isn't just about collecting aid; it's about strategically combining different forms of aid to stretch every dollar. For example, by combining a scholarship with a state-funded disability benefit, you can cover tuition and necessary living expenses, reducing financial stress. Additionally, consider applying for disability accommodations at work or school, which can significantly reduce daily living costs. Simple adjustments, like reduced transportation costs through paratransit services or subsidized housing options, can free up funds for other essentials. The key is to make your financial aid work together in the most efficient way possible.

Here are some inspiring examples. Sarah utilized a combination of a vocational training grant and a private scholarship designed for adults with autism, allowing her to complete her certification in graphic design without the burden of debt. Then there's David, who tapped into SSDI benefits alongside a part-time job, managed through a work accommodation that included flexible scheduling. These cases aren't just success stories; they're blueprints you can modify and apply to your financial strategy.

Navigating the world of financial aid for adults with autism doesn't have to feel like an uphill battle. With the correct information, careful planning, and strategic application, these resources can provide substantial support, opening up a world of opportunities. So, gear up, get organized, and start unlocking the financial aid doors that can lead to a more stable and fulfilling future.

As we wrap up this exploration of financial aid options, remember that each step in securing support bolsters your finances and contributes to a broader goal of empowerment and independence. You're not just navigating funding but investing in your future, one application at a time. Now, let's discover how to leverage your unique skills and newly secured resources to carve out a path to success in the professional world.

CELEBRATING STRENGTHS AND SUCCESS

Imagine stepping into a room where every story echoes triumph, every corner is lit with achievements, and every face you meet is a beacon of inspiration. Welcome to Chapter 8, where we toast the big and small victories of adults with autism across various fields. This isn't just a pat on the back; it's a resounding cheer for the heights reached when potential meets opportunity.

SUCCESS STORIES OF ADULTS WITH AUTISM IN VARIOUS FIELDS

Diverse Professional Achievements

We will begin with a spotlight on those who have turned their autism into a triumph in the professional arena. Picture Dr. Lena, for instance, who navigated the intricate world of neuroscience. With a mind that naturally patterns complex information, she's pioneered research reshaping how we understand brain connectivity. Dr. Lena's journey wasn't without hurdles—peer misunderstandings, sensory overload in busy labs, and the relentless pressure to communicate her findings in ways that didn't always align with her thinking style. Yet, her persistence and unique perspective led to groundbreaking discoveries and paved the way for more inclusive research practices.

Then there's Carlos, a software development genius whose knack for coding led him to develop an app now used by millions. For Carlos, code is poetry, and problem-solving is an art. His workspace confirms his need for a sensory-friendly environment: dim lights, noise-canceling headphones, and schedules that respect his flow states. His success story is a compelling reminder that accommodating individual needs doesn't just support the individual—it enhances the entire company's output.

Personal Achievements

Venturing beyond career triumphs, let's celebrate personal milestones that resonate with profound significance. Emily conquered her fear of public transportation, dramatically expanding her world and independence. Her journey involved meticulous planning, gradual exposure, and a support system cheering for every small victory. Today, Emily travels to volunteer at an animal shelter twice a week—a commitment that brings her immense joy and a sense of purpose.

Jordan's passion for cooking led him to master various culinary skills, and his sensory sensitivity turned into a palette for gourmet flavors. Cooking was once daunting, overwhelming Jordan with the kitchen's smells and chaos. Now, he hosts a small dinner club, where he shares his culinary creations—a testament to turning challenges into triumphs.

Impact of Support Systems

None of these stories would be complete without acknowledging the robust support systems that play a crucial role. For Dr. Lena, her mentor adapted communication methods to suit her processing style, providing feedback through detailed written notes instead of spontaneous verbal critiques. Carlos's success was bolstered by a workplace that not only embraced his neurodiversity but actively sought his input on creating more inclusive HR policies.

These support systems—whether family, friends, mentors, or colleagues—are there to assist and affirm that the challenges do not overshadow the individual's capabilities and potential.

Lessons Learned

From each story, a lesson can be gleaned. Dr. Lena's tale underscores the importance of perseverance and finding your niche where your traits are accommodated and celebrated. Carlos' experience highlights the transformative power of a supportive work environment that values diversity of thought and approach. Emily's journey teaches us about the empowerment of facing and overcoming personal fears. Jordan's story reminds us that our most significant challenges can sometimes lead to our most passionate pursuits.

Each narrative is a thread in the vibrant tapestry of success, woven from challenges overcome, barriers broken, and dreams achieved. As we celebrate these stories, let us draw inspiration and gather strength from their journeys, reminding ourselves that with the proper support, understanding, and opportunities, the sky is not the limit—it's just the beginning.

CREATIVE EXPRESSIONS: ART, WRITING, AND MORE

Let's paint a picture, not just with brushes and palettes but with words, music notes, and every hue of expression that dances across the autism spectrum. For many individuals, art becomes more than a hobby; it's a vital form of self-expression, a way to communicate inner thoughts and feelings that might otherwise remain locked away. Imagine the canvas as a silent companion that doesn't demand words but eagerly absorbs every color you throw at it, transforming your sensory experiences and emotional undercurrents into visual splendor. This art is a conversation without the clutter of words, where colors and shapes do the talking.

Consider the story of Clara, a painter whose abstract murals have turned city walls into open sky. Diagnosed with autism at a young age, Clara found verbal communication a challenge, often feeling lost when it came to social cues and expectations. Painting, for her, was a way to express her emotions and connect with others on a profound level. Each stroke was a word, each color a sentence. Her exhibitions showcase her talent and invite viewers into her world, offering a glimpse of the landscape through her eyes. Clara's journey underscores the transformative power of art as a means of communication, bridging gaps between her inner world and the outside, often misunderstood, world.

Music and writing serve similar purposes, offering alternative vocabularies for feelings and experiences that might be too complex or overwhelming to capture in everyday language.

Therapeutic Benefits of Creative Activities

Creating—whether art, music, or writing—carries profound therapeutic benefits. It's like having a personal therapist who doesn't judge or demand but encourages and listens. Engaging in creative activities can significantly reduce stress, providing a focus and flow that draws you away from the chaos of overstimulation and anxiety. It's a moment of control in a world that often feels unpredictable and overwhelming.

Moreover, the process of creating can enhance emotional regulation. It teaches patience, provides a sense of accomplishment, and can help process complex feelings. Art, music, and writing allow for the safe exploration of emotions, serving as outlets for frustration, sadness, joy, and everything in between. This kind of expression can boost self-esteem and foster a positive self-image; it's hard not to feel a surge of pride when you step back and see what you've created, a piece of your inner world made visible and beautiful.

Encouraging Creativity

You might be thinking, "But I'm not an artist." The truth is that creativity isn't about skill levels; it's about expression. Start where you are with what you have. Doodle, strum a guitar, write a poem, or rearrange your room. It's not about creating masterpieces; it's about mastering peace. Explore different mediums and activities until you find something that feels right and feels like you. And remember, every creator starts as a beginner. Every artist has a portfolio of unseen practice pieces. Give yourself the grace to be imperfect, learn, and grow.

To foster your creativity, consider joining a class or a workshop. This can be an excellent way to learn new techniques and connect with a supportive community of others who share your interests. Many communities offer art, music, or writing classes tailored to various skill levels and needs. These can provide structured opportunities to explore your creativity in a supportive environment, often with accommodations to make the experience more accessible and enjoyable.

Creativity in autism is a vibrant mosaic of experiences, a spectrum of expressions where every color, note, and word tells a story, turning the personal into the universal. Whether through the brush, the pen, or the piano, art in its myriad forms offers a powerful means of communication and connection as an artist, a creator, or a storyteller. So go ahead, pick up that paintbrush, that pen, or that instrument. The world is waiting to hear your story.

ENTREPRENEURSHIP: LEVERAGING INNOVATION

The entrepreneurial spirit of individuals with autism often means meticulous attention to detail, an ability to hyper-focus, and a knack for thinking outside the box (or smashing it completely). Where what some may see as hurdles, you transform into springboards for innovative solutions, offering an inspiring and appreciative unique perspective.

Let's chat about those unique qualities, shall we? In the world of startups, where one oversight can mean the difference between a product's success and its downfall, solid attention to detail is something that every venture needs. Then there's your ability to focus intensely on tasks for prolonged periods, often called "hyper-focus." This can be an incredible asset when developing new products or solving complex problems that would leave many others running for the hills. Innovative thinking enables you to develop solutions and ideas that zig while others zag.

Of course, the path of entrepreneurship is not without its brambles and thorns. Many entrepreneurs face significant challenges, from the social dynamics of networking to dealing with the sensory overload from busy work environments. But here's where your problem-solving prowess comes into play. Solutions like virtual networking events can help you build connections without traditional conferences' overwhelming hustle and bustle. For managing sensory challenges, strategies such as creating a tailored workspace that accommodates your sensory needs can turn a potential minefield into a productive sanctuary.

In entrepreneurship, having autism isn't just a footnote in your business plan; it's a core part of your competitive edge. View your characteristics as strengths that drive innovation and creativity. So, whether you're dreaming up the next big tech revolution or planning a venture that brings your passions to life, remember that in the bustling market of sameness, your unique perspective is not just valuable—it's indispensable.

CONTRIBUTIONS OF AUTISM THOUGHTS TO SOCIETY

Picture a world where every invention, discovery, and service is touched by the unique perspectives individuals with autism bring to the table. This unique cognitive approach has led to solutions and innovations that might never have been considered in a neurotypical framework. For instance, in the tech world, where precision and attention to detail are prized, autistic thinkers have engineered robust and more intuitive software for users who might struggle with more commonly designed interfaces. These contributions are filling gaps and redefining how we interact with technology daily.

In research, the meticulous nature of many individuals on the spectrum lends itself beautifully to fields requiring intense focus and a keen eye for patterns others might miss. There are stories of scientists working in genetics whose ability to sift through massive data sets leads to breakthroughs in understanding complex diseases. Their work doesn't just push the boundaries of scientific knowledge; it opens doors to new treatments and therapies that can transform lives. Imagine the ripple effect of such contributions —each discovery advances science and deepens our understanding of the human condition, showcasing the profound impact of including diverse neurological perspectives in research endeavors.

Now, shifting gears to community services, think about the grassroots movements powered by individuals keen on advocating for change. Their firsthand experiences with the challenges of navigating a world not designed for them fuel their passion for creating more inclusive, understanding communities. From leading initiatives that promote neurodiversity in the workplace to developing programs that help young people with autism harness their potential, their advocacy efforts are nothing short of revolutionary. These movements fight for rights and recognition and educate society, fostering a culture where diversity in neurological conditions is accepted and celebrated.

The impact of individuals with autism in these arenas underscores their invaluable contributions to societal development. It's a testament to what can be achieved by accommodating and embracing different ways of thinking and perceiving the world.

Integrating these unique perspectives makes society richer, more diverse, and more innovative.

Innovative Thinking

Consider how the focus and depth of interest that many autistic individuals possess can lead to a level of expertise in their chosen fields that few can match. This isn't just about having a job or a career; it's about igniting a passion that burns brightly enough to light up new paths of discovery and understanding. Whether it's developing new software that revolutionizes how we work or diving deep into climate change research, the contributions of these minds often lead to innovations that make the world a better place and a more interesting one to live in.

Prominent Figures

Highlighting the achievements of prominent individuals with autism helps to shatter stereotypes and inspire others. Take Temple Grandin, for example, whose innovations in livestock handling have revolutionized the industry by providing insights into animal behavior that have broad implications for welfare and ethical treatment. Her ability to see the world through a different lens gave her the empathy and understanding necessary to develop systems significantly reducing animal stress during handling.

Then there's Daniel Tammet, a savant whose extraordinary mathematical and linguistic abilities have set records and helped others see the potential for genius within the spectrum. His books and talks provide a window into the autistic mind, demystifying its workings and celebrating its capabilities, encouraging a shift in perception from focusing on limitations to exploring possibilities.

These individuals are exceptional because of their achievements and ability to challenge and expand our understanding of what it means to think differently. Their lives and work remind us that innovation doesn't always come from thinking bigger but often from seeing differently.

Advocacy and Change

On the advocacy front, adults with autism are leading the charge. They're at the forefront of movements that challenge outdated perceptions and push for policies recognizing the rights and potentials of people on the spectrum. Their advocacy is informed by personal experience, fueled by a desire for change, and strengthened by their resilience. They're not just asking for inclusion; they're demonstrating why it's essential for everyone.

These efforts pave the way for a future where being different is accepted and valued. They show us that the spectrum isn't a limit but a different vantage point that can lead to a richer, more diverse society. Perhaps most importantly, they teach us that the drive for change isn't just about altering policies and shifting attitudes but also about opening minds and embracing the full range of human diversity.

Valuing Diverse Perspectives

This celebration of diverse perspectives is crucial for those on the spectrum and for society as a whole. When we include individuals with autism in our communities, workplaces, and research teams, we're not just doing the right thing ethically but enriching our collective human experience. We're gaining access to ways of problem-solving and creativity that would otherwise be lost to us. We're learning that the keys to innovation and progress are as much about how we think as they are about what we think about.

The contributions of individuals with autism to society are profound. They remind us that our strength as a community lies in our diversity and ability to co-create. They challenge us to think not just about the contributions that individuals can make but about the contributions that might be missed if we fail to provide the support and recognition that allow these individuals to thrive. In celebrating their achievements, we acknowledge the potential for a more thoughtful, compassionate, and infinitely more creative society.

THE ROLE OF SPECIAL INTERESTS IN PERSONAL GROWTH

Defining Special Interests

When discussing special interests in the context of autism, we're not just talking about hobbies like collecting stamps or knitting cozy sweaters for chilly winter nights. However, those can certainly be part of it. Special interests often manifest as deep, passionate engagements beyond casual pastimes. They are intense, focused passions that absorb attention, provide immense satisfaction, and can sometimes evolve into vast reservoirs of expertise.

This enthusiasm is not just a hobby; it's a lifeline. For many, engaging with a particular interest is not just a pastime; it's a source of structure, comfort, and a profound sense of competence. It's a respite from the sensory and social challenges of daily life. Whether it's the intricacies of a programming language, the nuances of train schedules, or the migratory patterns of monarch butterflies, these interests are not mere distractions. They are therapeutic, offering joy, purpose, and a pathway to mastery.

Personal Development through Special Interests

The immersion in special interests can lead to significant personal development. Dedication to an area often cultivates an impressive and highly specialized skill set. This mastery can boost self-esteem and self-efficacy, demonstrating capability that might contrast with areas of life where these individuals may face challenges. For instance, consider someone whose particular interest is vintage automotive restoration. This field demands historical knowledge, mechanical skills, and meticulous attention to detail. The expertise gained here can be a source of personal pride and a professional asset, opening doors to career opportunities in restoration workshops, museums, or even roles as a consultant for film productions seeking authentic vintage car representations.

Moreover, engaging with a particular interest often involves problem-solving and innovation. When deeply invested in an area, you're likely to encounter challenges that require creative solutions—finding a rare part for a vintage car or coding a new feature for a software program. These challenges serve as mini-training sessions for the brain, enhancing cognitive flexibility and adaptability. They teach resilience and perseverance as the reward of advancing in your interest often requires overcoming obstacles and setbacks.

Social Connections through Shared Interests

One of the most powerful aspects of immersing oneself in a particular interest is the potential to forge connections with others who share your passion. Special interests can be incredibly niche, which might make it seem like they're isolating. Still, in reality, they often serve as bridges to communities of like-minded individuals. Online forums, clubs, and conventions can all be venues where individuals with similar interests gather to share knowledge, exchange ideas, and celebrate their common passions. These spaces can be particularly welcoming, offering a social circle where members are valued for their expertise and enthusiasm rather than their adherence to conventional social norms.

For example, imagine you are sincerely interested in medieval European history. Online communities and historical reenactment groups provide information and engagement with your interest and a social framework structured around shared activities and clear common goals. These settings can reduce the ambiguity and unpredictability of typical social interactions, making them more accessible and enjoyable. They offer a sense of belonging and validation that can be hard to find elsewhere, particularly for those whose interests stray far from mainstream topics.

Encouraging Exploration and Support

For families and supporters of adults with autism, recognizing and supporting special interests can be a game-changer in the individual's personal and professional growth. It all begins with understanding—acknowledging that these passions are not mere fixations to be tolerated but integral parts of their cognitive and emotional landscape. Support can take various forms, from providing materials and resources to engage with the interest to facilitating connections with experts or communities that share the same passions.

Providing support in exploring and nurturing their special interests also means being open to these evolving or changing interests. What may start as a fascination with the drawing could transform into an interest in animation or graphic design? The key is maintaining an open dialogue and actively listening to what the individual finds compelling and why. This support fosters their growth in practical skills and knowledge. It strengthens your emotional bond, demonstrating a profound respect for their interests, experiences, and identity. This adaptability in supporting evolving interests fosters a sense of autonomy and self-discovery.

We recognize and nurture special interests' role in personal growth and celebrate a core component of many lives. We acknowledge the joy, refuge, and profound engagement they provide. We open the door to a world where these passions are accepted and embraced as powerful catalysts for development, connection, and fulfillment.

FUTURE VISIONS: EMBRACING AUTISM'S POTENTIAL

What lies ahead for autism in the future of our society? Imagine a world where autism is as widely accepted and integrated as any other human trait, where support systems are not just available but are tailored so finely that they feel like a second skin. This isn't just wishful thinking; it's a possible future toward which we're steadily paving the way with every small victory and each giant leap forward in understanding and acceptance.

Futuristic Perspectives on Autism

A society where every autistic individual receives personalized support that flexes to fit their needs throughout their life. What a concept! We're not just talking about support in schools or workplaces but a continuous, evolving support system that adapts to life changes, including aging or transitioning between life stages. Imagine technologies not yet invented that could offer real-time cognitive or sensory support seamlessly integrated into daily life, maybe through devices that look as ordinary as a pair of glasses but function as a high-powered computer, providing sensory filters or communication aids as needed.

The integration of individuals with autism will likely go beyond mere inclusion. Future societies could celebrate neurodiversity as a standard principle, as biodiversity is essential for a healthy ecosystem. This shift could influence everything from policy-making to everyday social interactions, embedding the value of neurodiverse perspectives in the fabric of society. It's about crafting a world where everyone is accommodated and actively sought out for their unique viewpoints and skills, particularly in solving complex global challenges where lateral thinking is crucial.

Potential Developments in Technology and Therapy

On the tech front, the horizon looms with potential. We're already seeing the beginnings of AI and machine learning, which are helping to customize learning environments for students with autism or apps that assist with social interactions. Looking ahead, we could see the development of neuroadaptive technologies that interface directly with the brain, enhancing communication abilities for nonverbal individuals or modulating sensory processing to reduce overload in real-time.

Therapeutic approaches are also set to evolve, moving away from trying to make individuals fit into a neurotypical mold toward therapies that respect and enhance their way of experiencing the world. These therapies might involve virtual reality environments that allow individuals to simulate and practice interactions or control sensory input in ways that are currently unimaginable. The goal? To empower, not overwrite. It's about therapies that build on strengths rather than diminish them.

Empowering the Next Generation

By embracing and advocating for autism acceptance, pushing for innovations in technology and therapy, and educating society about the strengths of neurodiversity, we are setting the stage for a future where individuals can thrive. This empowerment will enable them to carve out paths that previous generations might have found impassable.

Consider the impact on the next generation of children growing up in a world where their potential is recognized and nurtured. These children may lead the way in fields like environmental science, where their unique skills can help tackle climate change, or social justice, where their inherent fairness and attention to detail can drive reforms.

Calls to Action for Society

What can we as a society do to fuel this progress? First, continue to advocate for policies that recognize and protect the rights of individuals with autism. Second, support research not only into autism but also into innovations that make life more navigable for people who have autism. Third, educate others about autism, break down myths, and foster a culture of acceptance and understanding.

Every blog post shared, every supportive policy enacted, and every technology developed with neurodiversity in mind adds bricks to the foundation of a more inclusive future. Taking proactive steps today will ensure that the society of tomorrow values and celebrates the potential within each individual.

Together, we can forge a future where autism is not just accepted but embraced as a vital part of human diversity, where the potential of all individuals is acknowledged and sought after, and where every new technology or therapeutic approach makes the world a more navigable place for everyone on the spectrum. It's a big dream, sure, but every reality starts as a dream, and every future begins with the vision we hold today. As we close this chapter, let's carry forward this vision, this relentless hope, into every action we take, building a bright future with the potential of every individual.

In wrapping up, we've envisioned a future where autism is integrated into the fabric of society with grace and respect. Let's carry this vision forward, applying it not just to autism but to all aspects of human diversity, exploring how each thread of our individual experiences enriches the tapestry of our shared human story.

CONCLUSION

We are at the end of our shared journey through *Essentials of Adult Autism.* I hope you've found a friend in these pages, a bit of a guide, and maybe a good laugh or two along the way. From the beginning, the mission was clear: to empower you—yes, you sitting there with this book in your hands (or on a screen)—by diving deep into the world of adult autism. Together, we've explored the challenges and the immense strengths and potentials that come with your unique wiring.

We started by laying the groundwork—understanding what adult autism means beyond the stereotypes. We discussed the importance of self-understanding and the sheer power of knowing oneself. We also discussed how crucial it is to find your people—those folks who get it—and the strength that comes from community and support. Whether it was navigating the tricky tides of workplace dynamics or the intimate dance of relationships, we tackled practical strategies to help you along the way.

And yes, we celebrated—you and all the incredible adults whose talents paint our world with brilliant colors and ideas. From those who transform challenges into innovations at work to those who turn personal passions into impactful ventures, their contributions are nothing short of essential to the fabric of our society.

As we close this chapter, I urge you not to see it as the end. Let it be the launchpad for your ongoing adventure. Advocate for your needs, seek out your community, and never stop exploring the vast potential that lies within you.

Remember, understanding and navigating autism is not a destination—it's a continuous journey. Stay curious, stay open, and keep learning. New strategies, new friends, and new opportunities are always around the corner.

Thank you from the bottom of my heart for walking this path with me. While our experiences might differ, this journey has bound us together in exploring the landscape of adult autism. You are not alone in this. We are in this together each step of the way, supporting each other through the challenges and celebrating every victory, no matter how small.

As we part ways, I leave you with a vision of hope—a future where adults with autism are more than accepted and celebrated for their unique perspectives and skills. Imagine a world where your abilities are recognized and where each of us has the opportunity to live a life rich with purpose and joy.

The world is richer for having you in it, just as your presence has immeasurably enriched this book as a reader. Keep turning the pages of your story, and remember, every day holds the possibility of a new chapter full of hope, growth, and connection. Let's keep making it a good one together.

Thank you for reading "Adult Autism Essentials." Your support means a lot and helps spread the word about the strengths and successes of adults with autism.

How Can You Help? After reading the book, I would love to hear what you think! Please write a review and share your thoughts. Your review can help others learn about the book and understand how it can help them.

* * *

Write Your Review Today!

Just scan the QR code or click the link below:

https://www.amazon.com/review/review-your-purchases/?asin=B0D94FDVN4

Remember:

- Share what you learned.
- Talk about how the book helped you.
- Be honest and kind.

I sincerely appreciate your feedback and hope this book positively affects your life!

Jason Jones

REFERENCES

1. ASERT. (n.d.). Be well, think well: Supporting individuals with anxiety and autism. PA Bureau of Supports for Autism and Special Populations. https://paautism.org/resource/be-well-anxiety-autism/

2. Autism, Altogether. (2017, March 19). Autism-friendly transport practices. Altogether Autism. https://www.altogetherautism.org.nz/autism-friendly-transport-practices/

3. Autism Speaks. (n.d.). Autism grants for families. https://www.autismspeaks.org/autism-grants-families

4. Autism Speaks. (n.d.). Employment rights. https://www.autismspeaks.org/tool-kit-excerpt/employment-rights

5. Autism Speaks. (n.d.). Financial planning tool kit. https://www.autismspeaks.org/tool-kit/financial-planning-tool-kit

6. Autism Speaks. (n.d.). Finding your community. https://www.autismspeaks.org/finding-your-community

7. Autism Speaks. (n.d.). Resources and services for adults with autism. https://www.autismspeaks.org/resources-autistic-adults

8. Beyond Akeela. (2023, May 2). A timeline of the neurodiversity movement. https://beyondakeela.com/2023/05/02/a-timeline-of-the-neurodiversity-movement/

9. Bronze, M. de, Evans, K., Whitehouse, A. J. O., Wray, J., Eapen, V., & Urbanowicz, A. (2022). Exploring the experience of seeking an autism diagnosis as an adult. Autism in Adulthood: Challenges and Management, 4(2), 130–140. https://doi.org/10.1089/aut.2021.0028

10. Building Design + Construction. (2018, January 25). Four keys to designing autistic-friendly spaces. https://www.bdcnetwork.com/blog/four-keys-designing-autistic-friendly-spaces

11. Davis, H. (2021, August 25). Adults with autism - What to say in a job interview | Adult Autism Center. Adult Ability Center of Lifetime Learning. https://adultautismcenter.org/blog/adults-with-autism-what-to-say-in-a-job-interview/

12. Davis, H. (2021, July 15). Autism and executive function | Adult Autism Center. Adult Ability Center of Lifetime Learning. https://adultautismcenter.org/blog/autism-and-executive-function/

13. Eby, E. (2024, April 5). Embracing neurodiversity: 6 incredible autistic artists to follow | Limitless Blog. Boundless. https://www.boundlesslife.com/post/embracing-neurodiversity-6-incredible-autistic-artists-to-follow

14. El Baou, C., Bell, G., Saunders, R., Buckman, J. E. J., Mandy, W., Dagnan, D., & O'Nions, E., et al. (2023). Effectiveness of primary care psychological therapy services for treating depression and anxiety in autistic adults in England: A retrospective, matched, observational cohort study of national health-care records. The Lancet Psychiatry, 10(12), 944–954. https://doi.org/10.1016/S2215-0366(23)00291-2

15. Ghanouni, P., & Quirke, S. (2023). Resilience and coping strategies in adults with autism spectrum disorder. Journal of Autism and Developmental Disorders, 53(1), 456–467. https://doi.org/10.1007/s10803-022-05436-y

16. Golden Steps ABA. (2023, December 16). Family dynamics and autism: Tips and strategies. https://www.goldenstepsaba.com/resources/family-dynamics-and-autism

17. Hiki- A social community & dating app by and for Autistic adults. (n.d.). Friendship and love for the autistic community. Hiki, Inc. https://www.hikiapp.com

18. Indeed Editorial Team. (2024, March 4). Networking for introverts: 7 tips for making better connections. Indeed. https://www.indeed.com/career-advice/career-development/networking-for-introverts

19. Integrated Autism Service. (n.d.). Understanding executive functioning difficulties. https://autismwales.org/wp-content/uploads/2020/09/10-Skills-for-Life-Handout.pdf

20. Jones, K. (2016, October 16). Autistic employees can give companies an edge in innovative thinking. The Guardian. https://www.theguardian.com/sustainable-business/2016/oct/17/autistic-employees-can-give-companies-an-edge-in-innovative-thinking

21. Koegel, L., Ashbaugh, K., Navab, A., & Koegel, R. (2016). Improving verbal empathetic communication for adults with autism spectrum disorder. Journal of Autism and Developmental Disorders, 46(3), 921–933. https://doi.org/10.1007/s10803-015-2633-0

22. Miller-Merrell, J. (2024, March 12). 27 companies who hire adults with autism. Workology. https://workology.com/companies-hiring-adults-with-autism/

23. Moller, R. (2023, November 13). Social skills training for autism spectrum disorder. Above & Beyond Therapy. https://www.abtaba.com/blog/social-skills-training

24. National Autistic Society. (n.d.). Anxiety. https://www.autism.org.uk/advice-and-guidance/topics/mental-health/anxiety

25. Office of Disability Employment Policy. (n.d.). Accommodations. U.S. Department of Labor. https://www.dol.gov/agencies/odep/program-areas/employers/accommodations

26. Pagni, B. A., & Braden, B. B. (2021). Early reflections on the therapeutic effects of mindfulness-based therapies in adults with autism and suggestions for future research. Journal of Psychiatry and Brain Science, 6, e210013. https://doi.org/10.20900/jpbs20210013

27. Reid, S. (2024, February 5). Adult autism and relationships. HelpGuide.org. https://www.helpguide.org/articles/autism-learning-disabilities/adult-autism-and-relationships.htm

28. SingHealth. (n.d.). Coping with sensory processing issues. SingHealth Group. https://www.singhealth.com.sg/patient-care/conditions-treatments/coping-with-sensory-processing-issues

29. Steyn, J. (2023, September 22). The unique strengths of autistic individuals in the tech industry. LinkedIn. https://www.linkedin.com/pulse/unique-strengths-autistic-individuals-tech-industry-johan-steyn

30. The Art of Autism. (2018, March 22). Organizations that support autistic entrepreneurs. https://the-art-of-autism.com/directory-of-programsstudios/

31. Zauderer, S. (2023, December 13). Legal advocacy for autism: What you need to know. Cross River Therapy. https://www.crossrivertherapy.com/autism/legal-advocacy-for-autism